Stoke next Guildford

A SHORT HISTORY

Stoke Church

Stoke next Guildford

A SHORT HISTORY

LYN CLARK

Phillimore

1999

Published by
PHILLIMORE & CO. LTD.,
Shopwyke Manor Barn, Chichester, West Sussex

ISBN 1 86077 122 X

Printed and bound in Great Britain by
BOOKCRAFT LTD.
Midsomer Norton

Contents

For
Winifred
Aylwin
and Nig

Good Companions

List of Illustrations

Frontispiece: Stoke Church

Acknowledgements

Without Shirley Corke, former Archivist-in-Charge in Guildford Muniment Room, this short history would never have seen the light of day. She pointed me unobtrusively, but firmly, in the right direction whenever necessary and I am immensely grateful.

When Chaplin's shop in North Street, Guildford, closed in the early '60s a large number of glass negatives were found ranging from the 1860s to the 1930s. Eric Hunter has used his skills to make prints and slides from the negatives which now constitute the Chaplin Collection in Guildford Museum. Eric has given many talks based on these slides and he has now found several negatives of Stoke next Guildford and has made prints both of these (labelled Eric Hunter's Collection) and of other pictures for this short history. His illustrations make an invaluable contribution to the book and I am very grateful to him for all the time and trouble he has taken to produce them.

Stoke's Tithe Map of 1841 is, like the parish itself, very large and complicated and without Anne Bowey's valuable help I should still be floundering.

The typing has been in the expert hands of Sheila Elliott and her team and I want to thank them particularly for their patience in fitting in a number of second thoughts.

As soon as the Surrey Advertiser book *Images of Guildford* was published I contacted David Rose to ask if I might make use of some of his pictures, particularly Woodbridge House and the Rectory Guest House. He kindly allowed me to do so and also to use the policeman postcards.

I am grateful to Dr. Alan Crocker for allowing me to include the sketch of Stoke Paper Mill drawn by himself from a larger picture in the Minet Library; and to Guildford Museum for providing the outline of the boundaries of the parish and manor of Stoke and for allowing me to use illustrations from the Museum archives.

I would also like to thank Walter Willcox for the trouble he took to photograph memorials and Dennis May for his drawings of Joseph's Road houses and Stoke Malthouse.

Mary Mackey and Duncan Mirylees, now both in the Surrey History Centre, have arranged for photographs to be taken of documents and maps in the Surrey History Collection. The following illustrations are reproduced by permission of Surrey History Services: 31, 32, 51, 52, 53 and 81.

I want to take this opportunity to thank Duncan Chappell of the National Portrait Gallery for tracing portraits of Jeremiah Dyson and of James Stirling, and Sheila Elliott for trying to obtain copies. Unfortunately they have not arrived in time but it is good to know they exist.

Finally, I would like to thank a number of people who were persuaded to read the text and to comment on it, particularly Shirley Corke, Mark Sturley, Audrey Monk, Dennis Turner, Mr. and Mrs. Penycate, Sir Edward Britton, Mary Alexander and the Rector of Stoke, who has also suffered several photographic invasions of his church without complaint. This list makes me realise how much invaluable assistance I have received from so many people. (Needless to say, errors are mine.) I am very grateful to all of them and to everyone who has helped me.

Introduction

The extraordinary thing about Stoke next Guildford is that, although it has been almost completely devoured by its neighbour, it still manages to retain something of its identity and to preserve evidence of its survival. The evidence is there in the parish church, in Stoke Park, in the Parson brothers' almshouse, in the mills by the river, in the earliest lock of the Wey Navigation, in Joseph's Road with its 16th- and 17th-century houses, in the timber-framed houses and sturdy cottages and terraces that line much of Chertsey Street, Stoke Road and Stoke Fields.

This study is not a definitive history of Stoke. To begin with, it does not deal with Stoughton which, in the Domesday Survey, was part of the manor of Stoke and which remained part of the parish of Stoke until the end of the 19th century. But the history of Stoughton has already been dealt with by the Rev. Henry J. Burkitt: *The Story of Stoughton by Pen and Camera* (1910), and by Anne Sankey: *Stoughton, Guildford People and Places* (1991), and so it will only appear peripherally in this short history. The writer's aim is to trace the history of those parts of Stoke which still exist before they disappear or are ever more completely hidden under a barrage of cars and housing estates and all the utilities which Stoke's neighbour has found it convenient to plant in Stoke: a leper hospital, a mad house, a workhouse, a cemetery, a barracks, a fire station, a sewage works, a lido, a technical college, a football ground, first one and then two by-passes and finally a Sports and Leisure Centre.

There are many unanswered questions in the history of Stoke. Was it of older origin than Guildford? Had it a Minster church? Why should it later become the head of an extensive Rural Deanery? What exactly happened in 1627 when Guildford Corporation asked that Stoke above Bars and Stoke Lanes might be included in the borough, received the King's assent by Letters Patent which later disappeared, while Stoke continued to control both areas until well into the 19th century?

Stoke has been adept at hiding the solution to these mysteries. Only one of its Court Books survives—that covering the years from 1772-1811, although there must have been Stoke Court Books going back to medieval times. The parish registers survive only from 1662. The boundaries between Stoke and Guildford have been complicated from the beginning and the Ichnography of 1739 sets more problems than it solves. Why was the small borough of Guildford surrounded by a manor many times the area of the borough, a manor which jealously defended its boundaries? Later came the time when the borough half swallowed its encompassing neighbour, creating Stoke Within and Stoke Without and making it almost impossible to use the early census returns to work out the population of Stoke—or Guildford.

The quiet village in the water meadows where a ford carried an ancient north/south road across the Wey has disappeared. The small country estates and farms that surrounded the village have also gone. To the west lay Woodbridge Park, the home of the Mangles family, M.P.s for Guildford, and close by was Woodbridge House where Colonel Manwaring Ellerker Onslow lived. To the east, behind the church, on rising ground was Stoke Park Mansion where the

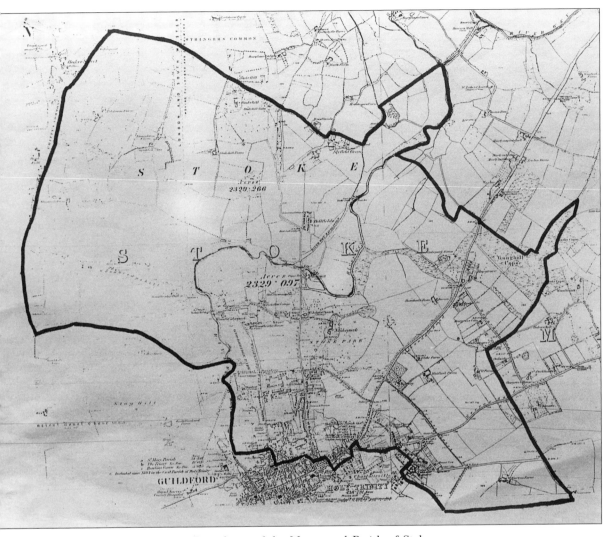

1 Boundaries of the Manor and Parish of Stoke

Delaps lived for fifty years. To the north stood Stoke Hill House, the home of the Paynters for a century. Behind these small estates lay the farms. Many of them survive only as names for residential areas: Glebe Court, Pit Farm Road, Watford Close, Ganghill. Three retain their identity: Burchatt's Farm, its timber-framed barn preserved for use as a social venue; Stoke Park Farm (originally the ancient Aldham, later Oldham Farm), now in Abbot's Wood; and Warren Farm, where the medieval manor courts of Stoke were held. Why there?

So while much of Stoke has disappeared, the problems of its origins, its boundaries and aspects of its history remain.

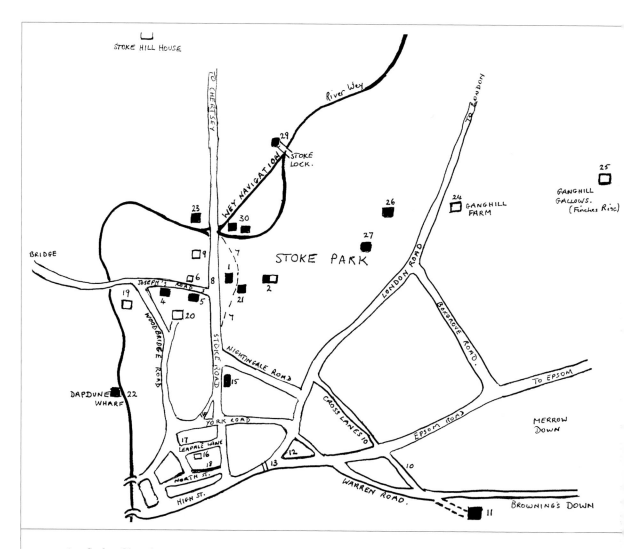

1. Stoke Church
2. Stoke Park Mansion
3. Joseph's Road
4. Virgeloes
5. Middleton Onslow's house
6. Joseph's wheelwright's shop
7. The old 'low, hollow way'
8. Aldersey's new road
9. Stoke Parsonage
10. Cross Lanes
11. Warren Farm
12. Site of Leper Hospital and Poyle House
13. Stoke above Bars
14. Stoke Fields
15. Parsons' Hospital
16. Leapale House
17. Leapale Lane, formerly Mad House Lane
18. North Town Ditch
19. Woodbridge Park, home of the Mangles
20. Woodbridge House
21. The Lido
22. Dapdune Wharf
23. Row Barge Inn
24. Ganghill Farm
25. Ganghill Gallows
26. Stoke Park Farm, formerly Aldham's Farm
27. Burchatt's Farm
28. Stoke Hill House, home of the Paynters
29. Stoke Lock
30. Stoke Mills

2   Diagram map of places mentioned in the text

One

Early History

Neolithic Settlement?

A contributor to *The Surrey Archaeological Collections*[1] writing in 1893, Frank Lasham, describes a 'very interesting core of flint. This was dug up at Stoke and is very similar in shape to cores of obsidian; it is perfect'. Nearly a century later numerous worked flints were found in the area near the Fire Station.[2] These would appear to show that the valley of the Wey attracted Stone-Age settlement as it was later to attract settlement in Saxon times.

Saxon Stoke

A glance at the map outlining the boundaries of the Parish of Stoke-next-Guildford shows that it was a large parish divided almost exactly in half by the River Wey. This was unusual as rivers normally marked the division between parishes. In the case of Stoke, while the parish remained almost exactly the same in acreage from Saxon times until the second half of the 19th century, the area sometimes split into two manors, one each side of the river, Stoke to the south and east of the Wey and Stoughton to the north and west.

The name Stoke comes from the Saxon word 'Stoc' whose original meaning was simply 'place',[3] probably a defensive place.[4] Such a basic name needed some extra designation to differentiate it from other Stokes: Stoke sub Hamdon and Stoke St Gregory are two of the many Stokes in Somerset, and in Surrey there is Stoke d'Abernon and Stoke-next-Guildford.

An Early Minster?

That Stoke existed in Saxon times is proved not only by its Saxon name but also by its probable Minster status. By mid-eighth century most of the English kingdoms had established a network of Minsters, covering five to 15 modern parishes and served by itinerant priests from the central church. John Blair suggests that Stoke may have had Minster status as Stoke Church stood on a royal manor and was farmed separately.[5] However there is no trace of mother church rights over neighbouring parishes such as the Minsters of Woking and Godalming had. Blair therefore suggests that Stoke, like Southwark, 'may belong to the category of "Burghal Minsters", originating with the re-organisation under Alfred and his successors'.[6] Whatever Stoke's status, there is no doubt that there was an early Christian settlement at Stoke which almost certainly pre-dated the first Guildford parish of St Mary's, but while St Mary's church retains some visual evidence of its Saxon origins the church of St John the Evangelist at Stoke has not been so lucky.

Domesday

The third, incontrovertible piece of evidence that Stoke had Saxon origins is that it is listed in William the Conqueror's Domesday Survey of 1086, where the value of the manor in the time of Edward the Confessor is given. Translated, it reads:

The King holds Stoke (-by-Guildford), in lordship. It was in King Edward's revenue. Then it answered for 17 hides; they paid nothing in tax. Land for 16 ploughs. In lordship 2 ploughs; 24 villagers and 10 smallholders with 20 ploughs. A church, which William holds from the king in alms with ½ hide. 5 slaves. 2 mills at 25s; meadow, 16 acres; woodland, 40 pigs; it is in the King's Park. Value before 1066 and later £12; now £15; however, its holder pays £15 by weight. The Sheriff has 25s.

Thus the whole of Stoke with its church and mills was in the direct possession of the Crown.

The Rev. Henry Burkitt points out[7] that the Manor and Parish of Stoke have altered very little in extent between the Domesday Survey and the Ordnance Survey map of 1870. The

Rex ten̄ in dn̄io STOCHÆ. De firma regis .E. fuit. T̄c ſe defđ p̄. XVII. hiđ. Nichil geldaueꝛ. T̄ra.ē.XVI.caꝛ. In dn̄io ſunt II.caꝛ. 7 XXIIII. uilti 7 x. borđ cū. XX. caꝛ. Ibi æccła.q̄ Wilts ten̄ de rege cū dimiđ hida in elemoſina. Ibi.v.ſerui. 7 II.molini de. XXV. ſol. 7 XVI. āc p̄ti. Silua: XL. porc̄. 7 ipſa.ē in parco regis. T.R.E. 7 poſt: ualb̄. XII. lib̄. Modo: XV. lib̄. Tam̄ qui ten̄ redđ. XV. lib̄ ad penſū. Vicecom̄ h̄t. XXV. ſoliđ.

3   Domesday Book entry for Stoke

plough was the amount of land which could be cultivated each season by one plough drawn, normally, by eight oxen. The hide was the Saxon version of the Norman plough. The area differed in different counties, varying with the nature of the soil. In Surrey, the hide or plough was about one hundred acres. Thus in Stoke there were 2,000 acres worked by villagers and smallholders, 200 held by the manor farm, 16 acres of meadow and 50 acres of glebe. This amounts to 2,266 acres but does not take into account the woodland for 40 pigs which lay within the royal park. The difference between this and the number of acres shown on the Ordnance Survey map of 1870 is minimal. In 1870 the number given is just over 2,329; in 1086, 2,266 plus.

However, the Domesday Survey is a complicated document and my thanks are due to Dennis Turner for pointing out that the Domesday Book hide is the fiscal hide and does not translate directly into acres of arable. There is also doubt about the area of woodland required for 40 pigs. Taking these considerations into account, it is likely that 11th-century Stoke was even more extensive than its later boundaries suggest. It certainly stretched from Warren Farm in the east to Worplesdon in the west and was almost wholly arable. There was very little wasteland in Stoke, which is unusual in Surrey.

Manorial Courts on the Downs

Until 1205, the manor of Stoke remained in the hands of the King with its church in Stoke and its manor house across the river in Stoughton. In 1205, King John sold the manor to the Bishop of London to raise money for his war with France. The price was 100 marks in cash and 100 shillings a year. At some time during the 13th century, Stoughton became a separate manor. Perhaps the Bishop of London sold Stoughton to the then head of the Stoughton family, founded, according to Sir Nicholas Stoughton in his *Collections relating to the family of Stoughton*, by one Godwin. Sir Nicholas describes his ancestor, alive in 1265, as Lord of the Fee, so perhaps Stoughton had separated from Stoke by then. At all events, Stoke remained in the hands of the Bishop of London and lost its manor house, while Stoughton was an independent manor but remained in the parish of Stoke. Since the Bishop of London never resided in Stoke, the manorial courts which supervised the administration of the manor were held at Warren Farm, over in the south-eastern corner of the parish on Browning's Down, near the top of Warren Road. There is still a Warren Farm there but the Domestic Buildings Research Group report that this is basically a 17th-century house with later additions and alterations. However, both Senex (1729) and Rocque (1768) label the area New Warren, suggesting that there was an earlier house. The Courts being held up at Warren Farm would help to account for Cross Lanes, that strange trackway running between steep banks up on to Browning's Down, perhaps made or at any rate used by the people of Stoke as they plodded up the long slope to the Warren to attend the Court Leet (for the election of officials such as the constable and the aletaster) and the Court Baron (to record changes of ownership and inheritance fines). If only one of the Stoke medieval Court Rolls had survived! But unfortunately there is only one survival and that, a late one, covers the years 1772-1811. Why this remote outpost on Browning's Down should have been chosen it

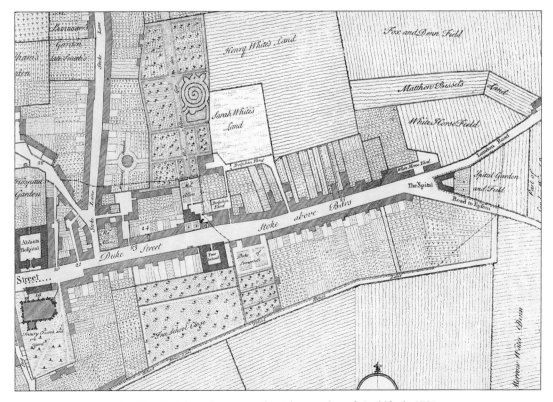

4   The Spital as shown on the Ichnography of Guildford, 1739

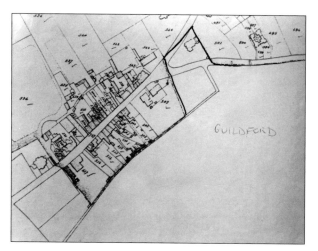

5 The Guildford boundary extended to include the Spital on the Tithe Award map of 1841

is impossible to say. Perhaps it was convenient for the Bishop's representative, if for no one else. It remained the headquarters for the manorial business of Stoke until 1615, when the Courts left Warren Farm for a place which came to be called Court Close, near the Parsonage.[8]

Lepers

Another medieval institution stood in the angle where the London and Epsom Roads fork at the end of what is now called Upper High Street. The old boundary of the borough of Guildford ran just to the east of the Royal Grammar School and crossed the Upper High Street to the east of the new building where Allen House used to stand. The boundary marker is still there. Above that point, the street was known as Stoke above Bars, and the area where the road widens for the fork was called the 'Spital. This is clearly marked on the Ichnography or Ground Plan of Guildford of 1739. In 1895, on the O.S. 1:2500 map, the length of the road between the Grammar School and the fork is marked Spital Street and the site of St Thomas's Hospital is shown. From the Ichnography, it is clear that this area lies in Stoke above Bars but a close look shows that the boundary line not only runs west along School House Lane but also east towards the road to Epsom and, crossing that road, surrounds the area of the Spital, Spital Garden and Field. A similar kink in the boundary between Guildford and Stoke is shown on the Tithe Award Map of 1842. The area clearly did not belong to Stoke, although territorially it seems it should have done.

This building, carefully kept at arm's length by Guildford, was the leper hospital. Conclusive proof of this is provided by the Calendar of the Liberate Rolls. I am grateful to Mary Alexander of Guildford Museum for drawing them to my attention. These rolls contain the record of pensions and other allowances made under the Great Seal: in 1249 and on several occasions in the years following, the King ordered the Sheriff of Surrey to pay the wages of 'two chaplains ministering in the chapel of the King's Castle of Guldeford and one in the hospital of St Thomas in that town to have 50s. each yearly for their wages'.[9] In 1257 there is a significant change: 'To the Sheriff of Surrey and Sussex ... to let the King's three chaplains of Gudeford, two celebrating in the king's court there and the third at the leper hospital outside Gudeford have their wages of 50s. each yearly from this Easter so long as he is sheriff'.[10] Mary suggests that the hospital may have been founded by Henry II soon after St Thomas à Becket's death in 1170. As the King paid the wages of the chaplains, it was almost certainly a royal foundation.

At the time this hospital was built, towards the end of the 12th century, the manor of Stoke still belonged to the King, who presumably saw no reason why a leper hospital for the royal borough of Guildford should not be built on land in the royal manor of Stoke.

The extraordinary thing is the long duration of this foundation. It probably ceased to be a leper hospital towards the end of the 14th century as leprosy had died out in England by then, but it remained to give its name to the Upper High Street until the end of the 19th century—Spital Street and the site of St Thomas's Hospital are both marked on the 1895 O.S. map 1:2500.

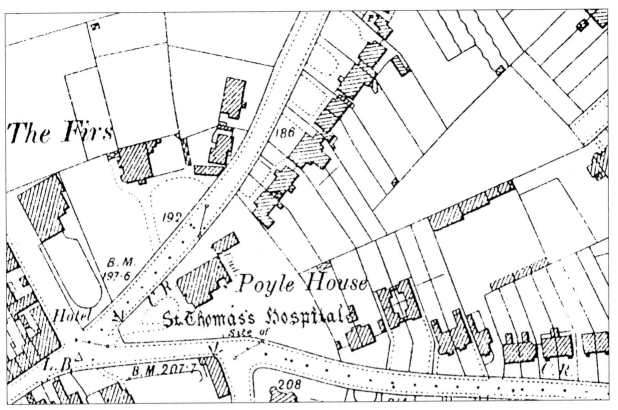

6   St Thomas's Hospital and Poyle House on O.S. map 1895

The Manor of Poyle

Also marked on this map is Poyle House. The Poyle estate originated in the ancient manor of
Poyle granted by William the Conqueror to Robert Testard.[11] In 1254 Thomas de la Puille held
a serjeancy in Guildford by a grant from Richard Testard. This was originally held by the service
of looking after the kept women of the King's Court but by 1254 was held by an annual rent
and valued at 100 shillings. When Walter de la Poyle died in 1299 the lands he died possessed
of were styled the Manor of Poyle and included land in Tongham and Chiddingfold as well as
in Guildford and Stoke. These scattered possessions represented the entire holding of the Testard
family, and the Poyle lands in Guildford and Stoke were obviously of some importance since
they also included the patronage of the Hospital of St Thomas. The site of this hospital was still
known in the 19th century as the map shows, and Manning and Bray write in 1804 of 'a small
building still to be seen here, adjoining the Epsom Road, which is manifestly of great antiquity
and was probably a chapel'. They also say, 'At present the Court Leet and the Court Baron of
the Manor of Poyle are annually held there'.[12] So the old Hospital of St Thomas became the
headquarters of Poyle Manor and of the Poyle Charity.

It would seem that the two manors of Stoke and Poyle existed in Saxon times. At the
Conquest the King took Stoke and gave Poyle to the Norman, Robert Testard. The fact that
these estates almost completely surrounded the small borough of Guildford suggests that the
borough was carved out of the two ancient manors. Poyle, because it passed to the Henry Smith

Charity in 1624, has disappeared territorially though its name can still be traced. The name Pewley is probably derived from Poyle Lea and there is a Poyle Road today, near Pewley Hill, all of which belonged to Poyle Manor. But the manor and name of Stoke survived until, in modern times, it was swallowed up by the small borough which it almost certainly pre-dated.

Soon after the foundation of the Hospital of St Thomas, the King sold the manor of Stoke to the Bishop of London and it remained in the Bishop's hands until 1559, when it reverted to the Crown under an act which recompensed the Crown for the loss of Tenths and other income from the Church. In 1587 the Queen granted it to Thomas Vincent of Stoke d' Abernon, and in 1589 he sold it to Laurence Stoughton for £1400.[13] The Stoughtons had held the manor of Stockton, Stoghton or Stoughton since before the manor of Stoke was separated from it. Now Laurence re-united the two manors and the Stoughtons remained Lords of the Manor throughout the 17th century until 1692, living in the manor house in Stoughton. They were supporters of Parliament during the Civil War.

Nicholas Stoughton, the author of the family history, was made a baronet only just after the Restoration, but the Puritan sympathies of the family continued into Charles II's reign and in 1683 Sir Nicholas was fined when his wife held a proscribed meeting at Stoughton Place. Sir Nicholas was very conscious of his family's long history and of himself he wrote: 'He himself, though nineteen heirs had intervened, at length succeeded.' Unfortunately he was to be virtually the last of his line. He died in 1686 and his son Laurence died without heirs in January 1692. The title died out and the Manor House at Stoughton Place was pulled down in 1700. The chief monument to the Stoughtons is their chapel in Stoke Church, and possibly also the mantelpiece in Guildford Council Chamber which may have come from the old manor house of Stoughton. (Note: In the context of Guildford, it is interesting that the reference in 1249 is to a castle. By 1257, the reference is to the Court.)

Two

The Parish Church

St John the Evangelist

The Building

Stoke Church has been altered and adapted over the centuries. As far as the building itself is concerned there may well be some Saxon foundations, although this has still to be confirmed. In 1985 an opportunity arose to see if there were any traces of the church's Anglo-Saxon origins. A concrete floor was to replace the wooden one and the Guildford Group of the Surrey Archaeological Society, directed by Dr. David Bird, was given permission to investigate when the wooden floor was taken out. Special attention was paid to the area between the columns of the north aisle arcade to see if there had been an original unaisled church. A large amount of flint rubble was found in that area and it is tempting to think that this was evidence of an Anglo-Saxon wall, but it could not be defined with certainty and there was no time for a more detailed examination. However, Dr. Bird has pointed out that if there was a wall between the columns it will have survived beneath the new flooring.[1]

The earliest parts of the existing building are the arcades of the nave and south chapel which are of early 14th-century date. The tower is late 15th century. It is built of chequered flints and local sandstone and has three stages with buttresses, a south-east turret staircase and an embattled parapet. The tower houses six bells. Three of them were cast at Eldridge's foundry at Chertsey and each bears the inscription: 'Bryan Eldridge made mee 1620'. The tenor bell was added in 1700[2] (a gift from the then lord of the manor, Edward Hubbald?), and two more given in 1954. The fifth bell was given in memory of Albert Shrubb and his wife Mary Ann, and the sixth in memory of Charlotte Bowyer and her husband William Paget

7 & 8 Lithographs of the west view and north view of Stoke Church published by H. Prosser, 1833

9   Interior of the church by H. Prosser, 1833

10   View of the church with cabriolet and parishioners, 1869

11   By the gate near the church, *c*.1875 (from Eric Hunter's collection)

Bowyer, churchwarden for 35 years. This ring of six bells is still in regular use.

The north chapel was probably added by the Stoughtons, who were then lords of the manor, towards the end of the 16th-century. There is no chancel arch. A cambered beam of late 16th century date supports the eastern gable of the nave. Pevsner picks out the east window as 'The best feature—the vigorous east window, an unusual design,—five lights with mullions running up uninterrupted into the head of the arch and deep concave splays inside and out', and he goes on to point out that the Stoke advowson was owned by the Priory of St Pancras, Lewes, 'the source for so many innovations in English medieval architecture'.[3]

In the 19th century there was much restoration and rebuilding. The north aisle was completely rebuilt and widened. The 20th century has seen further alterations, most noticeably the removal of the Victorian pews and gallery, the insertion of the new floor in 1985 and the building of a new church centre opened in 1981 and named after the founder of Western Australia who married Ellen Mangles of Woodbridge on her 16th birthday.

Rectors of Stoke

William was the name of the first recorded rector of Stoke Parish Church. His name appears in the Domesday Survey of 1086 where it is recorded that he held 50 acres of land directly from the King. The name William suggests Norman origin. John Blair writes: 'Royal priests were the most frequent recipients of valuable churches, and the unidentified William who held Stoke by Guildford church in alms may have been another cleric in the Conqueror's household'.[4] The site of the Saxon church is not known for certain but it seems likely that its position today on an outcrop above the River Wey crossing was also its original position.

St Pancras, Lewes

Stoke next Guildford was a royal demesne from the reign of Edward the Confessor until John sold the parish to the Bishop of London in 1205. However, the advowson, the right to appoint to a benefice which was a widespread means of patronage, appears to have been acquired by the Lewes priory of St Pancras in the 12th century. It is listed in Henry of Blois' 1160 Confirmation of the churches and tithe acquired by Lewes Priory in Surrey, where it is referred to as 'Stocka juxta Geldeford', but the Confirmation document does not name the donor. However, the King may well have bestowed the advowson on William, who became the fourth Earl of Warenne in 1148. He owned extensive estates in Surrey as well as in the Lewes area of Sussex and may have received the advowson in return for some service rendered to the King. The Earl may in turn have transferred it to St Pancras Priory. John Blair points out that in the 12th century there was a flood of possessions from the hands of laymen into those of the new religious houses and de Warenne's gift to Lewes Priory is an example of this movement.[5]

It is interesting to note from the Lewes documents that Stoke was still of some ecclesiastical significance. The witness list in a Lewes Charter of c.1160-80 begins with 'Gilbert decano, Godado presbitero, Rogero sacerdote de Stokes', which may possibly indicate a residual collegiate staff[6] (assuming that the 'Stokes' referred to was the Surrey Stoke).

The advowson remained in the hands of the Priory at Lewes until the Dissolution. In

12 An early postcard of the church, with policeman and old and young parishioners.

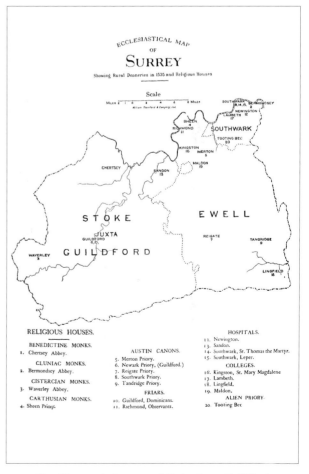

13 The rural deanery of Stoke-juxta-Guildford

14 Stoke Parsonage

1549 it was sold to Laurence Stoughton. When Rose Ive, daughter of Elizabeth Hammond and stepdaughter of William Hammond of Guildford, married the then Laurence Stoughton at the end of the 16th century, William was persuaded to give property in Guildford and East Horsley to his stepdaughter and her husband. In return, he and his wife received the advowson of Stoke for their joint lives with remainder to the Corporation of Guildford who were to appoint the Master of the Grammar School to the benefice of Stoke, thus helping the Grammar School by increasing the Master's income. It seems that Laurence's father, Thomas, did not actually have the power to give the patronage of Stoke away from the Stoughton family since he only had a life interest in it and his heir Laurence had not been a party to the transaction. In 1598 Laurence agreed that though the patronage was rightly his, he would not appoint to the Rectory at Stoke without the consent of the Mayor and Approved Men of Guildford.

Two Masters of the Grammar School were appointed under this arrangement: John Crowe (1598/9-1633), who was also rector of Holy Trinity Church in Guildford, a position he resigned on his appointment to Stoke; and William Hill (1633-62), who on his appointment resigned as Master of the Grammar School. These resignations seem to indicate that Stoke was a well-endowed benefice, certainly more valuable than Holy Trinity. A later Stoughton, Nicholas, in his will of 1647, tried to recover the advowson fully by substituting an income from other property in Claygate and Holy Trinity. This did not produce anything like the equivalent of the

Stoke advowson, although, very strangely, the Mayor and Approved Men expressed themselves satisfied and the right to appoint to Stoke returned to the Stoughtons. Perhaps the fact that the then schoolmaster, John Graile, was not in Holy Orders and was a cousin of Nicholas had something to do with it. It appears that John Hammond's attempt to help the Grammar School by giving it the patronage of Stoke did not succeed.[7]

When the last Stoughton died in 1691/2 the advowson went to the new Lord of the Manor of Stoke, Edward Hubbald, and then to the next owner of the manor, Nicholas Turner. John Russell bought it from the Turners and it was handed on to Russell's son in 1762. He died in 1766 and his family, all daughters, sold the advowson to George West, who appointed his son to the parish in 1795. Manning and Bray record that this George West 'has greatly improved the Parsonage House'.[8] George West continued in possession until Samuel Paynter took over in 1831. The work of the Paynters will be dealt with later (see Chapter 10).

This reference to the Parsonage House draws attention to another Stoke mystery. Why was the house where the rector of Stoke lived always known as the Parsonage? That the nomenclature was of long-standing is shown by references in the deeds of Watford House. In December 1570, John Smallpiece of Guildford, clothier, conveyed to Geo. Parvis of Watford, Stoke, yeoman, a '½ acre in Stoke Field next the Parson's Path'. In September 1571, there was an agreement for exchange when Geo. Parvis and Henry Stoughton of Woodbridge swapped a ½ acre next Parson's Field and a ½ acre in Stoke Field next Parson's Path.[9] That the Parson's Path linked glebe land with the church and parsonage seems probable but we do not know where the Parson's Field was, nor do we know why the rector was always known by the general term 'parson'. The only picture of Stoke Parsonage that we have is unfortunately not dated but looks of late 18th-, early 19th-century date.

15 The Old Rectory Guest House

David Rose of the *Surrey Advertiser* has drawn my attention to this postcard of the Old Rectory House and has kindly allowed me to include it. The card was posted on 22 September 1922 and the writer, Edgar, was enthusiastic about Stoke as a holiday centre, 'This is a fine spot for a holiday. Plenty of sport, rowing, good weather. Fine old house isn't it.'

So eventually Stoke Parsonage did become known as a Rectory. When the Paynters moved to Stoke Hill House (see Chapter Nine) the Parsonage was used for the curates of Stoke. There appears to have been a fairly rapid turnover (Robert P. Blake in 1841, William H. Stevens, 1851, etc) and Trollope could well have had Stoke curates in mind when he wrote of Mr. Quiverful.

Next there is the question of Stoke's place in the organisation of the church: possibly a minster in Saxon times, a royal parish under the Normans, possibly a collegiate foundation. And, at the Reformation, another change. The Valor of 26 Henry VIII recognises three deaneries in Surrey: Ewell, Southwark and Stoke, and of the three Stoke is by far the largest (see V.C.H. map).

From 1535 until 1878, Stoke-juxta-Guildford was Surrey's most extensive rural deanery. Whether this was due to Stoke having held a prominent position in the past, or to machinations at the Dissolution, or to royal whim, it is impossible to say.

The Parish Registers date from 1662[10] and in addition to the record of those who have been baptised, married and who have died in Stoke, there are also lists of 'those in the parish who received a certificate under the hands and seals of the minister and churchwardens that they might be touched for a disease called the King's Evil'.[11] At the back of the same register is an 'Account of Briefs'. These were Crown Licences to collect money for various charitable purposes. John Burscough, rector from 1662-1707, seems to have been the only rector conscientiously to keep a record of these collections and it is interesting to see where the money went. In 1682, 12 shillings and 10 pence was collected for Poland. 'Received of Mr. Burscough of Stoke next Guildford the sum of 12 shillings and nine pence being what was collected on the Brief for the fire in the Maze in Southwark' (the Maze was a Southwark manor). Also '£3. 12s. 5d. for ye Redemption of captives in Slavery ... ' Wolver (sic) Hampton and Milden Hall also received help from Stoke.

In addition to its bells and its Parish Registers, Stoke also has some communion silver. A silver paten and a silver flagon were given by the first Lord of the Manor after the Stoughtons had died out. On each there is an inscription: 'The Gift of Edward Hubbald Esq. 1702.' There is also a silver cup with the London hallmark of 1599, and a copy made in 1826 with the inscription: 'The offering of a few friends of Stoke Church 1826'.

Finally the church contains numerous monuments and memorials which together record the history of the Parish. The earliest mention of a memorial stone to be placed in Stoke Church occurs in the will of 'William Combes of Stoke nygh Guldeford Gent' dated 31 January 1500/1.

> To be buried before the Rood in Stoke Church ... Also I will that Anne my wife bring me conveniently to my long home ... I will that my executor do lay a stoane upon me within a year of my departing ... My brother Thomas shall have my train of oxen with the weyne and harness thereto belonging and my best horse and the half occupying of the ferme at Stoke during my years.

Probate for the will was granted in 1503.[12] Whether the stone was ever placed before the Rood in Stoke Church we do not know. But we do know that Edward Hubbald was buried near the high altar with a black marble stone recording that: 'Here lieth the body of Edward Hubbald Esq., who departed this life the 5th day of July 1707 in the 70th year of his age'. This memorial of one of Stoke's Lords of the Manor is no longer visible and there is another hidden memorial which Henry Peak, Guildford's Borough Surveyor (1864-92), records in his Note-book[13]: 'When engaged in carrying out some works there' (Stoke Church) 'I noted that the

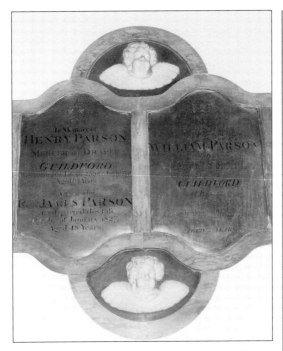

16 Memorial to the two brothers, Henry and William Parson, and their 'nephew'

17 *Right*: Harriet Aldersey's monument to her husband

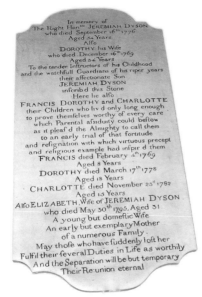

18 The Dyson memorial

19 Charlotte Smith's memorial high up on the north wall of the chancel

workmen having occasion to cut through a vault in the Stoughton Chapel (it was on the 17th October 1887) the remains of an elm coffin were exposed ... much decayed.' However there was also a brass plate which was engraved as follows:

> Futura Praeterites
> Jonathan Harris Turner
> Arm^{ge}
> Obit Jan^u 27 1747
> Anno Agens 33

J.H. Turner was Lord of the Manor from 1722-47. Near him in the same vault lay his mother who died 'in the 50th year of her age'.

The Stoughton chapel contains the memorials to the Stoughton family and also one to Jeremiah Dyson who succeeded the Turners as Lord of the Manor (1761-76). It was placed there by his son not only as a memorial to his parents, 'the tender instructors of his childhood and the watchful Guardians of his riper years', but also to his brother (died aged 8), two sisters (died aged 18 and 15) and his wife (died aged 31). This is a splendid example of an 18th-century inscription (see photo) and a reminder of the brevity of many lives at this time, or any time up to the 20th century.

20   The Hillier memorial

There are also memorials to William Aldersey (1780-1800), who changed the face of Stoke; to Nathaniel Hillier (1800-10), who succeeded Aldersey and collected ancient stained glass which he placed in an east window of the Stoughton chapel; to the Parson Brothers who built Stoke Hospital (or almshouses); to Charlotte Smith, who supported her large family by writing; to John Creusé, an important Stoke landowner, and Elizabeth Anne his wife; to Sir James Stirling, who founded Western Australia, and his wife Ellen Mangles; to Anne, the wife of Richard Budgett, son of yet another lord of the manor, Mr. James Samuel Budgett. Richard succeeded his father in 1906 but the death of his wife in 1888 at the age of 27 must have been a sad blow. Her memorial is a Pre-Raphaelite window in the north wall of the Stoughton chapel designed by F.J. Shields who was a friend of Rossetti and probably also of Richard Budgett. Finally, there are the memorials to Samuel Paynter and his son Francis Paynter, who managed the ecclesiastical affairs of the parish from 1831 until the end of the century (see Chapter Nine). The stained glass window in the tower bears the inscription: 'May 1893. In memory of the Reverend Samuel Paynter former rector of this Parish this window has been erected by his son and daughter, Francis and Julia Paynter.' In addition, there are two memorials which could be said to constitute a rogue's gallery: one is to James Price and the other to David Irish (see Chapters Eight and Twelve).

Three
Waterways and Mills

The Flowing River

On his father's death in 1613, Sir Richard Weston inherited Sutton Place. In part of his park the River Wey meandered through rich alluvial soil, but much of the remainder was on poor Bagshott sand, described by William Cobbett as 'rascally common covered with poor heath'. Sir Richard determined to do something about it. His solution was to bring water from the River Wey to irrigate his estate. This meant purchasing land through which his water channel could be constructed. His most important transaction was the 1,000-year lease of lands at Stoke from Sir George Stoughton in 1618. Weston secured the right to 'cutt, digg and make a trench ... through the lands and grounds' of Sir George Stoughton.

Between 1618 and 1620 Weston constructed a channel 8ft. wide, 4ft. 6in deep and 3 miles long, from Stoke Mills to Sutton Place.[1] By the operation of an experimental lock at Stoke the water level in the channel could be controlled, and during the winter months the water would be allowed to overflow, to float the water meadows on his Sutton estate. Thus came into existence the 'Flowing River' although it was not until 1631 that its purpose was described as being 'for the overflowing and watering of (Sir Richard Weston's) parke and lands adjoining'.

According to John Aubrey, this 'Flowing River' enabled 'six score acres of grounds to be flooded which before was most of it dry'. The land adjoining the Flowing River now yielded

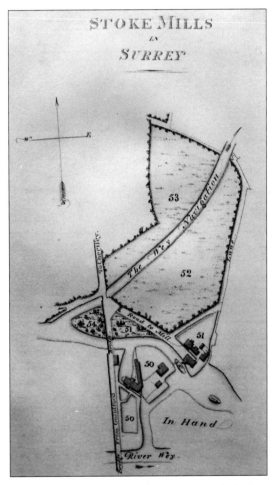

21 Stoke Mills as shown in Harriet Delap's (née Hillier) estate book (1812)

200 loads of hay more per year, and Weston told Adolphus Speed that 150 loads of 'his extraordinary hay which his meadows watered by his new river did yield were sold at near three pounds a load'.[2] Today the course of the Flowing River has been lost in the sewage works to the north and east of Stoke Lock, but can still be seen where it is crossed by the drive up to Sutton Place from the A3.

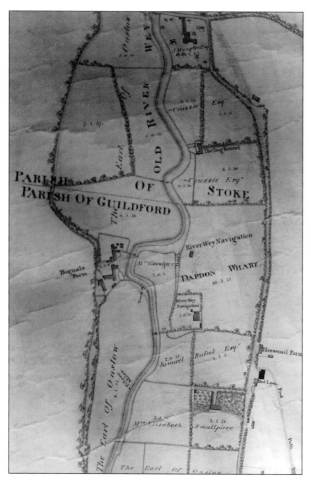

22 Wey Navigation map of 1823 showing Dapdon (Dapdune) Wharf and Cruzzie Esq.'s (John Creusé) property

Stoke Lock

Stoke Lock was the earliest of all the locks constructed on the Wey, built by Sir Richard Weston to control the water in the Flowing River. To begin with there may have been only one gate, but later with the new cut from Stoke Mill to the lock, a second gate must have been added, to make a new pound lock. The keeper's cottage is not the oldest on the Navigation because the site suffered from subsidence, being partly on banked-up ground. The lock was a dangerous place. The Parish Register for 1748 records (with a certain amount of ghoulish detail) Amos Tuck and Ann Ledier 'both drowned by accident below Stoke Lock. They were lovers. The young woman fell in and her lover endeavouring to get her out fell in also and both were drowned together'. Much the same must have happened on 28 April 1792, when the lock keeper died trying to rescue his daughter: 'William Punter and Jane his daughter from Stoke Lock drowned'.

In the heyday of the waterway there was barge traffic through Stoke Lock all the year round. Today, the busy time for the lock is in the summer, when narrow boats queue up to go through; but in winter there is very little traffic, except for work by the National Trust to keep one of the oldest navigations in England in a state of good repair.

Surrey's First Paper Mill

This was built at Stoke about 1635 by Sir Richard Weston at a time when the decline in the woollen industry was making fulling mills less profitable. The fact that Surrey had numerous fast-flowing streams, needed in the preparation of pulp (known as 'half-stuff') for paper, and London was within comparatively easy reach, meant that Surrey waterways and mills were well placed to develop a paper industry. London was a plentiful source of the rags needed to make paper and was also a profitable market for the finished article. Stoke Mill not only produced paper but also made the moulds—frames covered with a fine wire mesh—which were dipped into vats of pulp or 'stuff' and then hung up to dry in shuttered lofts. The only other known manufactory of moulds in Surrey was at Albury and that did not come into use until 1794. Dr. Alan Crocker gives the names of several paper mould makers of Stoke in 'The Paper Mills of Surrey'.[3] He also gives a picture of Stoke Mill based on an original drawing of about 1800, showing a tall building with shuttered lofts necessary for drying the paper. Not only was Stoke Paper Mill the first in Surrey; it was in use longer

23   Stoke Paper Mill, *c.*1800 (from Dr. Crocker, in *Surrey History* vol.IV, no.1)

than any other Surrey mill, from 1633 to 1835, after which it continued to make machine-made paper until 1869.[4]

The Wey Navigation

The Navigation was established because wooded Surrey was well placed to supply the rapidly expanding capital with many of the commodities it most urgently needed. But Surrey's roads in the 17th century were, still not much more than trackways through clay and sand, and were virtually impassable for heavy traffic. Unless alternative means were found, Surrey would miss the opportunity to supply London with all the timber, corn, flour and paper its insatiable appetite demanded. Thus the idea of a waterway to carry goods to the metropolis became more and more compelling, and there were several attempts to bring in legislation for making the River Wey navigable.

This account of the Wey Navigation owes an enormous amount to Shirley Corke, former archivist in the Guildford Muniment Room, who kindly lent me her book on the subject.

In 1621 and 1624 bills for 'prostrating weirs' upon the river were read and referred to the Committee stage in Parliament, and in 1641 a bill was introduced to promote a Wey-Arun canal, but these three attempts came to nothing. However, in 1635, Sir Richard Weston persuaded the Earl of Arundel to obtain a commission from Charles I which empowered any six of 24

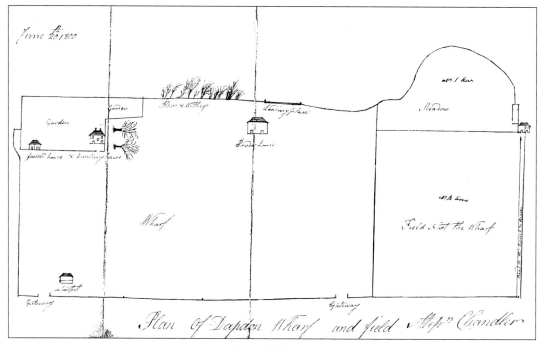

24   Plan of Dapdon Wharf and field, 20 June 1800

commissioners, of whom Sir Richard was one, to survey the river and carry out the work.[5] He immediately began negotiations with neighbouring landowners, until he was forced abroad by the Civil War.

On his return he pushed for an Act, which was passed on 26 June 1651, 'for Making Navigable the River of Wye'. This was an enormous undertaking, on a much larger scale, and with more interests involved than the Exeter Canal, its only precursor. Only 2½ years elapsed between the cutting of the first sod and the day when the first barge from Guildford entered the Thames. The speed with which this was achieved, plus the lack of any trained surveyor (because at this time such people did not exist— Sir Richard was his own surveyor) combine to account for the many difficulties, adjustments and legal suits which accompanied and followed the completion of the Navigation. That it was finished at all and so quickly is a miracle, particularly as a new Act had to be negotiated after the Restoration. Sir Richard died before its completion but there is no doubt that Stoke Mills and all the other mills along the Navigation benefited from his waterway (though he did not), nor any doubt that the canal was a tremendous engineering feat at that time; but there were mills like those at Byfleet that stood on the old river and could not reap the same benefits.

A Question of Wharves

A difficulty which became acute, especially for Guildford, was the siting of wharves, particularly as one of the commodities transported was gunpowder from the Chilworth Mills. At Stoke there was abundant room for a large wharf and it appears that Stoke was not slow to exploit this advantage. On 5 April 1654, Guildford presented a petition, signed by the Mayor and 26 others, claiming that as they had helped to procure the Act to assist the people of Guildford, there should be a place for landing commodities within Guildford. It was quite wrong for all other goods as

25 Stoke Mill with mill house behind (from Eric Hunter's collection)

well as timber to be unloaded on wharves in Stoke 'where the undertakers (canal managers) are now making them quite out of town whereby … it is manifest that they intend to take the whole business and accommodation from the said town of Guildford to Stoke and other places to the impoverishment of the said town'.[6] Eventually the Navigation acquired a house and wharf in Friary Street which became known as the Meal Wharf. Dapdune Wharf was leased to the Navigation, first by Pitson, fraudulently, and thereafter by successive owners of Woodbridge, until acquired by the Stevens family at the end of the 19th century. In the long run, Stoke did not cut out Guildford—quite the contrary. In the quarter ending 29 September 1775 (125 years after Guildford's original complaint) 1,425½ tons were loaded or unloaded at Guildford, at Stoke only 73 tons.[7]

Charges and Counter Charges

One difficulty was the attempt made by some landowners to make a personal profit from the canal trade. Extra charges such as that of 6s. 6d. at Stoke imposed by Sir Nicholas Stoughton, by far the most grasping of the landowners, led to a sharp falling off in the number of barges using the canal: in 1667-8 there were 314 barges, in 1671-2 only 84. Inevitably there were quarrels between canal users and mill users over available water, the bargemen needing to pen the water to work the locks and the millers needing a steady volume of water to work their

26 Stoke lock, *c*.1870 (from Eric Hunter's collection)

27   A boating party and traffic jam at Stoke lock (Eric Hunter's collection)

machinery. However, pressure for canal trade by users who found it invaluable for transporting goods, led to claims and charges being reduced or removed, eventually leaving only the 'undertakers' charge.

In 1671, by a statute of 23 Charles II, trustees were appointed, with power to settle claims from those who had suffered or were in debt as a result of the construction of the Navigation. For instance, Abraham Barnard of Stoke, paper maker, claimed £200 for water taken from his paper mills; and Henry Stoughton of Stoke next Guildford, yeoman, who owned a meadow called

> Woodbridge Mead in Stoke of about 3 acres and land called Sandyfields, now used as a wharf, claimed recompense for damage by bargemen and their horses, and by flooding, and for damage to the orchard belonging to his dwelling house by reason of the penning of the water there.[8]

As the Navigation approached Guildford from the north it ran through Stoke, so it appears from the claims that Stoke suffered more than Guildford from flooding and waste of water, etc. and very few of the claimants received any compensation. On the other hand Stoke's almost unlimited wharfage space was a great advantage in the early days of the Navigation.

Stoke Mills certainly benefited from the Navigation. Corn was unloaded at the Mill from the many farms round Stoke, and could then be reloaded as flour to go by barge to the great

28   Stoke Bridge (with policeman)   **29**   Stoke lock (with policeman)

'maw' of London. Timber from Surrey was in constant demand for the rebuilding of London after the Great Fire and for the expansion of the Navy. It was an unwieldy commodity most easily carried by water. Charcoal, a by-product of wood, might be carried in either direction, and pit or sea coal came up the Navigation in increasing amounts for householders in the Guildford area. Rags from London were unloaded at Stoke and manufactured paper returned by barge. Chalk for liming was another commodity which was transported by water. In 1670, Sir Nicholas Stoughton remarked that his Stoke fulling mill was used by 'all the country work from Bletchingly side and Godstone'.[9] Stoke was not involved in the loading of gunpowder from the Chilworth Mills. The gunpowder barges would have passed along the cut at Stoke but they were loaded at Dapdune Wharf, or later, at Stonebridge Wharf on the Godalming Navigation. But there was plenty of activity at the Mills. On the 30 December 1782, the *Sussex Weekly Advertiser* gave notice of Sale by Auction at Harraway's Coffee House, Change Alley, London, in January 1783 of Stoke Corn Mill, 'which is served by a valuable head of water, nearly 6ft. fall with two water wheels each 14ft. diameter which works three pairs of stones and six dressing machines, together with suitable buildings'. The penning of water for the convenience of barges was also mentioned and 'a new erected Saw Mill constructed on a curious principle ... to work by a 14ft. water wheel, 40 saws which are capable of cutting upwards of 5,000 superficial feet of timber per day'. Fortunately for the survival of Surrey timber, this did not become a permanent feature of Stoke Mills. *The Times* of 15 January 1814 recorded a sad event:

> A melancholy accident on Wed. morn. Jan 12 when Mr. Bart, a miller in the parish of Stoke near Guildford was drowned in his millpond. He was breaking the ice on and about the mill wheel when he fell into the water and perished. He has left a widow far advanced in pregnancy and nine children to lament his loss.

Between 1838 and 1847, the Magnay family, papermakers of Postford and Westbrook Mills, held Stoke and probably used the mill to make pulp or 'half stuff'. Then from 1852 the Pewtress family of papermakers took it over.[10] In 1863 it was destroyed by fire. The following account appeared in the *Sussex Advertiser* of 30 June 1863.

> Considerable excitement was occasioned in Guildford soon after 3o'clock on Thursday afternoon by announcement that the extensive paper mills ... had caught fire ... After what assistance could be obtained had been given, it was decided at last to send for the Guildford engine, but the people there, who were asked, refused to yoke their horses to it and finally it was pulled by hand; but it was 1½ hours before it could be brought to the scene by which time the mill was reduced to a heap of ruins.[11]

30   Stoke Mill today

Immediately after the fire in 1863, Henry Peak, who had already established himself in Guildford as architect and surveyor and who was to be appointed Borough Surveyor in 1864, was called upon to clear up the mess. He records in his notebook that he was 'employed to arrange the rebuilding of portions of the Stoke Mills, to put in turbines for water power and to adapt the works for paper mills'. The rebuilding started well and 'the foundation stone was laid by Mrs. Onslow'. However, 'a difficulty arose as to payment and the operations were stopped upon the failure of Mr. Wilkin the lessee'. Henry Peak adds, 'I had some difficulty to obtain from Mr. Wilkin the amount which I had paid for the nicely engraved silver trowel which he had requested me to procure for presentation to Mrs. Onslow'.[12] Dr. Crocker refers to 'a new single storey brick building (which) was soon erected and used as a "half stuff" mill'.[13] This must be the building that Henry Peak embarked on. However paper-making had ceased by 1869. Frederick and Henry Bowyer, who had taken over the corn mill in 1855 and in whose family it remained until 1938, decided to build a new mill in 1879 on the site of the old paper mill. It was designed by the architect H. Moon of Godalming. Beautifully prepared drawings for this large building still exist.[14]

At first the new corn mill was driven by a huge water wheel, and in 1893/4 it was converted to a roller mill. The water wheel was replaced by turbine in 1915 and the mill kept working until 1956. The oldest part of the site is the mill house which dates in part from 1650. One of the 1915 turbines stands on the bank near the mill, given by Grant & West (a chemical firm which took over the mill in 1957) who donated the turbine to the National Trust when it became responsible for the waterway in 1963. Later the site became part of a boatyard.

In 1989, Grant & West decided to put Stoke Mill out to rental tender and the Crown Prosecution Service moved in and is still there. There is plenty of space (about 15,000 sq.ft. of high quality office accommodation) and there is no air-conditioning. The absence of air-conditioning was one of the requirements of the Service—their aim, to avoid contracting legionnaires' disease.[15]

There have been mills at Stoke since before Domesday and it is good that the Victorian mills have been saved. They serve to remind us of their predecessors (as we view them through the feeder roads and the second bypass). The former bustle of commerce and water transport, of which the mills were the centre during the heyday of the Navigation between its opening in 1653 and the arrival of the railway in 1844, has disappeared (to be replaced by the roar of incessant motor traffic). The chief value of the Navigation today is as a picturesque waterway for recreation and 'messing about in boats'. Since this chapter was written, the Crown Prosecution Service has moved out and the *Surrey Advertiser* has taken over Stoke Mill, thus maintaining continuous activity on the site since Saxon times.

Four
The Village

The Tithe Award Map of 1842 shows very few houses near the church. It is impossible to say if this had always been so or whether the new road built by William Aldersey served to isolate the church. Manning and Bray wrote in 1804, 'It should not be forgot that Mr. Aldersey finding it necessary to take down some cottages in the course of his alterations, built new and neat ones in their room in an equally convenient situation'.[1] So far it has not been possible to pinpoint the whereabouts of these 'new, neat' cottages. The Senex map of 1729 and the Rocque map of 1768 both show the lane to Woodbridge with scattered buildings adjoining.

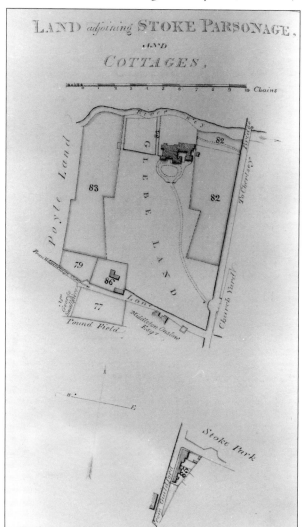

The Josephs

There is another map in Surrey History Centre showing 'Land adjoining Stoke Parsonage and cottages', an estate map of 1798, reproduced for Mrs. Delap, formerly Miss Harriet Hillier, in 1812.[2] They are identical in content although slightly different in execution. In addition to the Parsonage and a list of five tenements at 85, 86 is listed as 'J. Joseph. A cottage garden. Wheelwright's shop, etc. near the Pound'. There was a William Joseph giving evidence in the Bridge Inquiry in 1810, where he is described as 'aged about sixty has lived in Stoke ever since 11 years old. His grandfather a wheeler at Stoke, bound apprentice to him and served his time. Worked as a journeyman as long as his grandfather lived then took to the business and has carried on ever since'.[3] Finally, Stoke's only surviving Court Book, covering the years 1772-1811, records that in 1772 and 1777 William Joseph paid rent arrears for 'part of Black's house',[4] and that in 1777 he was also sworn in as one of the Jury. In 1803 he appears as Constable,[5] and in 1811, when James Copus, Pounder, did not appear, William Joseph was appointed Pounder as well as Constable.[6] It would seem that not only was there a

31 Plan of land and cottages adjoining Stoke Parsonage, from estate books of 1798 and 1812

wheelwright named Joseph (grandfather J. and grandson W.) on the road to Woodbridge for many years, but William Joseph was also a man with a position of responsibility in the community—a reliable chap. This gives William Joseph a strong claim to be the man after whom Joseph's Road (originally Joseph's Lane) is named. (Note: Every reference found so far is to William Joseph, so perhaps both grandfather and grandson were called William and 'J' has crept in, in error, from Joseph.)

Ancient Houses

The wheelwright's house and shop are no longer there but the house then owned by Mr. Middleton Onslow still exists. This is one of the oldest houses in the district and, considering its size and longevity, it is annoyingly lacking in documentary sources. According to John Baker,[7] the house was originally a farmhouse. Its nucleus is the wing to the west. To this was added a single newel post stairway. Then followed the rear block, which was the farmhouse kitchen, and the right hand stack served the kitchen fire and bread oven. There is no doubt that this part of the house dates from the 16th century because an open fireplace with Tudor brickwork has been found in the front room of the west wing. The timber lintel is concealed in the brickwork, but the Tudor bricks, wider and flatter, stand on edge in front of the timber and the hearth has been restored with Tudor bricks found in a wall in the garden where an old well has also been found.

32 Key to map, with J. Joseph the wheelwright and constable at No.86

Extensions to this Tudor house were added in the 17th century, when it is believed that the house became an inn. A large inn cellar remains under the western half. At some stage it may have again become a farmhouse. By the end of the 18th century, Mr. Middleton Onslow owned the property and by the 1840s it had been divided into three cottages. In the 1950s the property passed into the ownership of the Council and was converted into two residences. Mr. Penycate, who lives in the oldest part of the house and who found the well, points out that no house of any size would have been without its own well.

However this handsome house is not the only ancient house still in existence in Stoke. Further along Joseph's Road on the south side stand Nos.35 and 37 and I cannot do better than quote the report by Mary Butts after the house had been recorded.[8]

> This building in the ancient village of Stoke was at one time three cottages but Nos.35/37 have now been incorporated. The centre part of the house was, around 1500 or earlier, a hall house with evidence, which remains, of a smoke louvre. It was probably thatched at first and the rafters are

smoke-blackened. At a later stage, a smoke bay was inserted. Later still, the central chimney was built with an inglenook hearth beneath. In the 17th and 18th century extensions were added at the back and at each end, and the roof was tiled.

The medieval house had a hip and gablet roof, and framing in the upper front includes most of that for an oriel window to the open hall. There are arching braces up to the purlin in the centre bay. Other features include: long carpenters' marks in Roman numerals; an 18th century window cut through the wall plate with a strong iron bar bolted across it and its glass wired on to the iron mullion; a diagonal Georgian hearth in the corner of the 18th century extension and the remains of an early stair which was revealed near the inglenook hearth during recent work done in the house.

This house was most interesting to record and is an important example in the area of medieval domestic building, its date being somewhat earlier than that originally assigned to it.

33   Nos. 35 and 37 Joseph's Road, formerly Virgeloes, one of the oldest houses in Stoke

34   Nos. 9 and 11 Joseph's Road. Dennis May's impression of this range of 16th- and 17th-century buildings

35   Nos. 9 and 11 Joseph's Road

The history of this house can be traced for three centuries. In 1697, Augustine Darby sold to Edward Hubbald 'All that messuage … called by the name of Virgeloes or by any other name … and the gardens or orchards thereto belonging.'[9] The place seems to have been so well known, there was no need to describe its position. In 1698 Edward Hubbald released Virgeloes to Robert Figg of Stoke, miller. Between 1698 and 1772 the same property, still called Virgeloes, passed to Thomas Eager of Stoke, because in 1772 he sold the tenement and garden, called Virgeloes, to George Smallpiece of Stoke, yeoman. In 1802 John Creuzé acquired Virgeloes 'and also all buildings and gardens' from George Smallpiece. In 1826 John Creuzé's trustee sold the property to John Ottoway of Stoke-next-Guildford, gardener. In 1856 Virgeloes reappears, now divided into three tenements inhabited by Elizabeth Ottaway, widow, and John Smith of Stoke, builder; the third resident was Mary Moore. The property must have continued in the Smith family because, in 1948, a John Smith conveyed it to Surrey Equities, who in turn conveyed it to Marguerite Shuttleworth; fortunately, these title deeds were deposited in the Guildford Muniment Room.[10]

These examples of old houses in the vicinity of Stoke Church suggest that it was here that the village grew up, and Joseph's Road still retains the atmosphere of a village street. In the 18th century, open fields lay between this settlement round the church and the overspill from Guildford. In 1796, when William Parson completed the Almshouse planned by him and his brother Henry, a bell tower was necessary to summon help in an emergency, since there were no other houses anywhere near. However, in the 19th century this was to change. The enlargement of the 1870 O.S.6in. map shows that there was continuous development along Chertsey Street and that Stoke Hospital was no longer completely isolated. It also shows that it was not from the nucleus round the church that modern Stoke developed but from the overspill from Guildford along Chertsey Street and Stoke Road.

36   Old houses in Stoke by H.J. Sage

A Place in the Country

However, there is plenty of evidence that, until then, Stoke led a relatively independent existence and in addition to the village houses and their occupants, in the 18th century it also supplied prosperous Londoners with a 'place in the country'.

In the south east, property values were rising and it made sense to buy property as an investment. The construction of new bridges at Westminster and Blackfriars between 1739-50 opened up the Surrey side of the river for capital investment and for residence and there is evidence that Stoke became home to several prosperous lawyers and merchants.

One of these was Anthony Allen. Born in Hertfordshire, he went to Eton and King's College, Cambridge, and graduated in 1707. He became a lawyer and, with the support of Speaker Arthur Onslow, was made a Master in Chancery. Perhaps it was his friendship with Arthur Onslow that led to his buying property in Guildford and Stoke. His splendid house (later called Allen House, opposite the Royal Grammar School) stood just within the boundaries of the Borough of Guildford, but his equally splendid garden lay in Stoke (see the Ichnography 1739). The description of the boundary between Guildford and Stoke which accompanied the Ichnography can be found in Russell's *History and Antiquities of Guildford*, based on the 16th-century Guildford Court Book. It provides an interesting commentary on boundary lines between Stoke and Guildford—confusing to say the least.

'The jury upon their oaths say that the boundaries ... do begin between Master Allen's mansion house and brewhouse' and having circled Guildford 'keep close to the west side of Master Allen's garden wall and move directly south to the end thereof. Then turn up to the north east corner of his said house, pass by the chimney ... and go directly forward through the brewhouse belonging to the said house into the ... high street where you first began.'[11]

Anthony Allen became an Approved Man of the Corporation of Guildford and in 1740 became Mayor of Guildford. He was buried in the Temple Church in 1754.

Another inhabitant of Stoke was Francis Ketyllby. He had property in Middlesex and in Essex, and in 1750, the year of his marriage, he is described as 'of the parish of St Botolph without Aldgate'. At the beginning of the 18th century this was considered a good residential area but, as it became more crowded, it became less desirable and Francis was one of those who moved south of the river. In 1757 he bought property both in the parish of Holy Trinity, as an investment, and in Stoke as his own residence. The Stoke property is described as 'all that messuage … stable and a piece of ground … used as a garden or orchard situate in Stoke Lane in the parish of Stoke, adjoining the said lane on the west, the land now of Rebecca Allen, widow, on the east.'[12]   He continued to own property in Essex and in Whitechapel, but rural Stoke appears to be the place which became his favourite residence. He died in Stoke and his death is recorded in the Parish Register (12 April 1778) and in the obituary notices in the *Gentlemen's Magazine*. He left the property to his wife Mary, who in turn left it to their daughter Mary, who expressed the wish to be buried at Stoke 'beside her mother next the Church'. (The Ketelbey connection with Stoke was drawn to my attention by Miss C.D.M. Ketelbey, younger sister of Albert Ketelbey, in the course of her research into the many branches of her family.)

Another gentleman of substance connected with Stoke was John Creuzé, of Huguenot extraction, who came from London into Surrey in 1781 and in 1788 became High Sheriff of the County. He owned property in the Dapdune area and let Dapdune Wharf to the proprietors of the River Wey for 1,000 years for a timber wharf. On an early 19th-century map of the Wey Navigation his name appears as 'Cruzzie Esq.'[13] He lived at Woodbridge House and is buried in Stoke Church where there is a memorial to him and his wife on the east wall of the south aisle. A portrait of his wife by Gainsborough is in the Louvre.

But the most important of these men of substance and connections who settled in Stoke in the 18th century was William Aldersey. He radically altered the layout of the village and developed the park. His new road and new bridge were the most important developments.

The New Road and the Bridge

At this time Stoke Lane ran to the east of Stoke Church, going round behind it in a long curve and crossing two waterways, the first a tributary of the Wey, crossed by a small, ancient stone bridge, then the River Wey itself, crossed by a ford and a wooden bridge near the Mill. The old road is described on the map as being in a low, hollow way.[14] Even today, the ground drops away at the east end of the church, and then the lane would probably have been even lower, sloping down to river level from the church. The insertion of two by-passes across the area makes it difficult to envisage the sunken lane but if one looks at the drop behind the new *Parkway Hotel* and the water meadow below, it is possible to imagine how difficult it must have been to make one's way along the low, hollow way and across the fords and the two old bridges where the Wey often spread in flood water across the meadows.

Because of a later inquiry, to which frequent reference is made in documents in the Guild-ford Muniment Room,[15] there is plenty of evidence of the difficulties encountered. William Joseph, already mentioned, described as an elderly inhabitant, spoke of 'a hollow bad way and very swampy and sometimes waggons stuck for an hour or two'. He also mentioned that:

> Nicholas Turner, the then owner of the estate, was always quarrelling with Russell the Parson about the Tythe and he put a bar to the stone bridge to prevent the parson going over … John Harwood lived in the parish 70 years … had heard say that Mr. Stoughton built the bridge because his horses got chilled by going through the water to church and to Guildford.

The difficulty in crossing the Wey meant that Stoke and Guildford were virtually cut off from any reasonable volume of traffic and trade along the road which ran due north towards Chertsey.

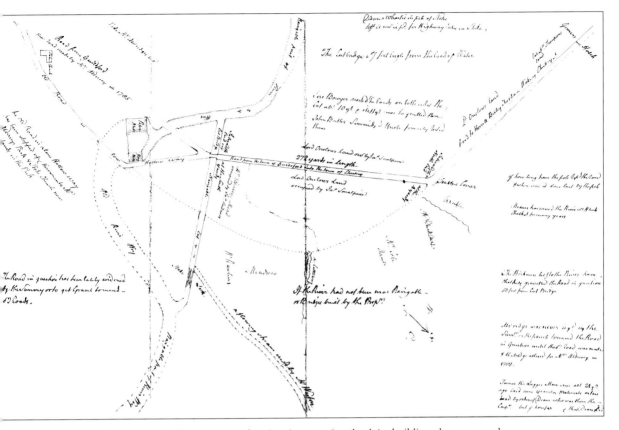

37 A rough diagram map showing interests involved in building the new road

William Aldersey altered all this. In a document, dated 26 May 1784, it was announced:

> And the said William Aldersey proposes to turn the road at his own Expense through his own land
> upon high ground which is not subject to be overflown and to make a New Road at his own Charge.
> And he also proposes to Erect a Brick Bridge for carriages and to give it to the Publick and to place
> it so as to meet the New Road. By which the Road will be made considerably shorter. And the new
> Bridge and New Road will be of great Public advantage.[16]

So obvious were the advantages arising from this proposal that the document goes on to
mention a list of subscribers 'willing to promote so useful a work', but unfortunately the list is
missing.

Aldersey bore the bulk of the expense of the project, but other interests were affected,
particularly the parish church and its glebe land. The new road would pass the church to the
west, thus making the church appear to be in the park and would swallow up a wide strip of
glebe land. This was one of the first points dealt with. A specially convened session of Justices
of the Peace, probably in 1784,

> do hereby order that the said highway be diverted and the surveyor of the highways for the said Parish
> of Stoke proceed to make agreement with the Rector and Patron of the Parish Church of Stoke,
> the consent of the Bishop of the Diocese being first had and obtained.[17]

The only plan of the change in the Guildford Muniment Room is the one that shows that
the New Road passing west of the church was 20 rods shorter and joined the old, bad, hollow

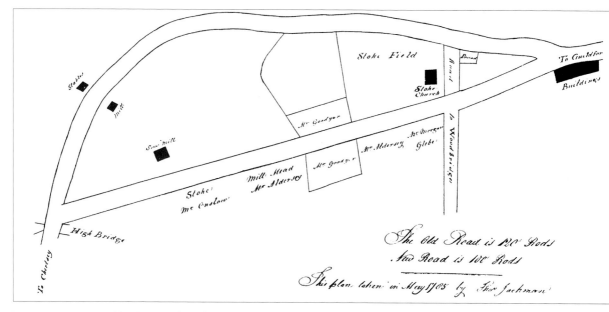

Stoke Field

To Guildfor

Stoke Church

Buildings

Stables

mill

Saw mill

Mr Goodyer

To Woodbridge

Mr Overgoe

Mrs Aldersey

Globe

Mr Goodyer

Mill Mead

Mr Aldersey

Stoke

Mr Onslow

High Bridge

To Chertsey

The Old Road is 120 Rods
New Road is 100 Rods

This plan taken in May 1785 by Thos Jackman

38   A neat plan of the old and new roads taken in May 1785 by Thos. Jackman

39   'The low hollow way' behind the church

road just before the high Cut Bridge over the Wey Navigation.[18] A bridge had been there since the construction of the Wey Navigation in the mid-17th century. Today it is still necessary to have three bridges to cross the Wey and its ramifications at this point.

The new set-up was completed in 1785 and it was agreed that:

> Mr. Aldersey made one of the best parish roads in the county, through his own estate and at his own expense built two excellent bridges at very great expense to make it a solid and level road so that there should be no water at flood times in any part of it ...

the result being 'that intercourse between Guildford, Chertsey, Woking and other places have been so increased since the new road and bridges have been made which could not have been in the old road'.

The Bridge

The gratitude felt towards William Aldersey was obviously immense and no controversy arose until after his death in 1800. Then there came the question of responsibility for maintenance of the road and bridges. They were so much

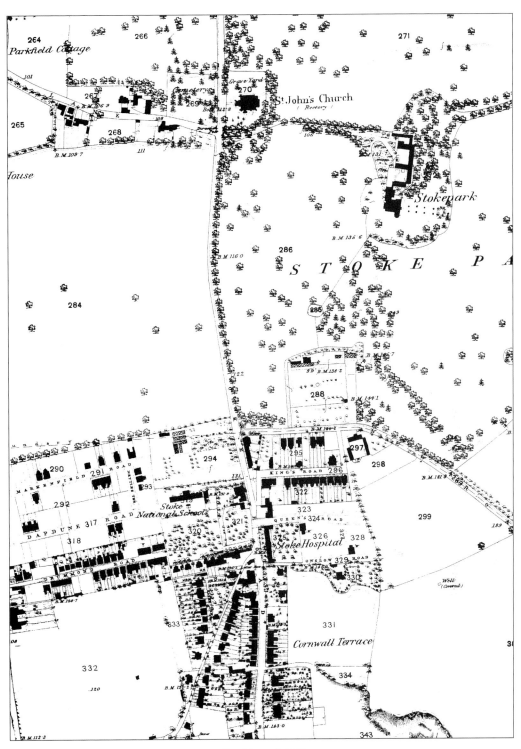

40 Map of 1869

41 Map of 1871

42   Some old (and new) houses in Chertsey Street

larger and so much more used than the old ones that the new owner of Stoke Park, Nathaniel Hillier, was reluctant to take on the much-increased maintenance costs. Out of this came the Inquiry which delved back into the pre-Aldersey past, and weighed up the results of the changes and a rough map was made of all the interests involved.[19] It was pointed out that Mr. Aldersey by 'banking up the water, thereby benefited himself as he was enabled to make ponds for the use of his paper mill', and also 'for the ornament and embellishment of his pleasure grounds'.[20] But the increased volume of water in a narrower channel led to the smaller of the two Aldersey bridges being swept away in 1809.

A committee was immediately appointed 'to consider the most eligible plan for repairing Stoke Bridge'. They met at the White Hart in Guildford and reported:

> We are of the opinion that a Bridge formed of one arch is, on account of the High Floods to which it will be exposed, best adapted to the situation. But we beg leave to add that we have received

43 Stoke fields has managed to retain the small 'country in town' atmosphere of the 19th century

information … that excites in our minds considerable doubt as to the liability of the County to maintain or repair the Bridge.[21]

With the weight of the evidence and opinion going against him, Nathaniel Hiller proposed that the cost of the repair should be paid jointly by him and the county without prejudice as to liability and the question as to future maintenance should be tried. The bridge was repaired jointly, but before the matter could be brought to trial, Mr. Hillier died in June 1810. In view of the doubts which had excited the minds of the earlier committee, it is slightly surprising to find, on 15 January 1811, 'Messrs. George and Job Smallpeice, contractors with this County' for keeping in repair 'several bridges including Woodbridge and two bridges at Stoke', asking the county for the money due to them for keeping in repair 'the parapets, walls, together with the roads over and approaches to the said bridges'. The county seems to have picked up the bill without any further fuss.[22]

Anyone who wishes to read in more detail of the arguments for and against the Lord of the Manor's liability for the bridge will find a fascinating collection of documents under the number 1320/16/21-50 in the Surrey History Centre.

The new road ran to the west both of the church and of the churchyard. This is shown clearly on the estate map of 1798 (see Chapter Nine). It ran through glebe land but permission for this was obtained from the bishop and no earlier burials were disturbed. Later on, the demand for burial space increased. It was therefore decided that the graveyard must be extended and the glebe land on the other side of the road provided the necessary space. It was here that Francis Paynter was buried (see Chapter Nine).

Five

Stoke Park, the Nabobs and their Successors

New Lords of the Manor

Because the King and later the Bishop had been Lords of the Manor but had never lived or visited there, Stoke had no manor house. From 1589 until 1697 the Stoughtons were the Lords of the Manors of Stoughton and Stoke and the manor house was Stoughton Place. However, when Edward Hubbald bought the estate in 1697 he demolished Stoughton Place, leaving the manor without a headquarters except for the manorial courts, which since 1615 had met not at Warren Farm up on Browning Down but at Court Close, adjoining the Parsonage.[1] Perhaps the new Lord of the Manor thought that Stoughton Place, some way across the river to the north and linked to the rest of the manor only by the low, narrow way which was often flooded, was too far from the church, the parsonage and the centre of the network of lanes which criss-crossed Stoke and which led west to Woodbridge, north-east to Dorking and south to Guildford.

The Hubbald estates are listed, and the Surrey History Centre has evidence that Hubbald consolidated his new possessions by buying and selling properties. They are listed in the Abstract of Title drawn up for Dyson, a later owner of the estate, probably after he had suffered a stroke in 1774 and wanted to have his affairs in order for his young son.[2] The Stoke estate included Woodbridge messuage and farm, Walnut Tree Close, Pound Close, 'And all that capital messuage Farm and Mansion House of Watford with the barns, stables, outhouses … orchards and gardens thereto belonging', and land adjoining Upper Cross Lanes and Browning Down. It also included

> All that messuage or tenement with barn, stable, orchard and one close of arable or pasture containing about two acres called the Vine Tree situated near Stoake Church between the King's Highway leading from Guildford towards Stoake Mill on the west part, a lane leading from Stoake Church towards Dorking on the north and the lands of Edward Hubbald on the east and south.[3]

It seems likely from the description of its position that the Vine Tree became the residence of the new Lord of the Manor. However, Edward Hubbald did not enjoy his new position for long. When he died in 1707 he was buried before the high altar in Stoke Church and was succeeded by his son William, who had been Paymaster and Accountant of the Navy Office and who outlived his father by less than three years. In 1711 arrangements were made to sell his estates to pay his debts and in 1718 the manor was bought by Nicholas Turner Esq. of Bignor Park and Hardham Manor in Sussex.

John Baker, in his article on Stoke Park Mansion,[4] praises the early 18th-century work found in the house, and it may be that the Turners did what the Hubbalds had intended to do and began to build a mansion house. There was a house on this site marked 'Esq. Turner' on Senex's map of Surrey (1729) so the Turners must have built something there between 1718-29, perhaps to take the place of the Vine Tree house. That something eventually took its place is shown by the note in the margin near the description of the Vine Tree messuage, which says 'This house was pulled down and laid into the lawn before the mansion house'.

This is not the only marginal note. It appears that William Bray, lawyer of Great Russell Street, and historian of Surrey, asked a solicitor, Mr. Holliday, for his comments on the Abstract

of Title drawn up for Mr. Dyson, to use as a
basis for the next owner's claims in Stoke
(William Aldersey's in 1781). Mr. Holliday's
comments were frequent. Of a long list of places
he wrote in the margin: 'These were not conveyed by Mr. Turner to Mr. Dyson and are
supposed to have been before sold by him', of
another; 'Sold by Mr. Turner before Mr.
Dyson's purchase'. It would seem that the
Turners sold off a considerable amount of land
but perhaps this was to enable them to concen-
trate on the mansion. That this may have been
so is suggested by Jonathan Harris Turner's will.
Nicholas Turner died in 1722 only four years
after his purchase of Stoke, and his elder son,
Jonathan Harris Turner, was only eight years

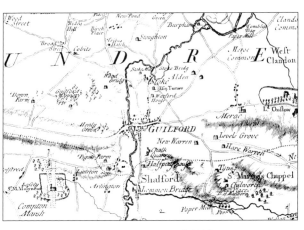

44   Senex map of 1729

old at the time. He himself died at the comparatively early age of 33, as the brass tablet found
in the vault under the Stoughton Chapel testified (see Chapter 3). However, the name of Turner

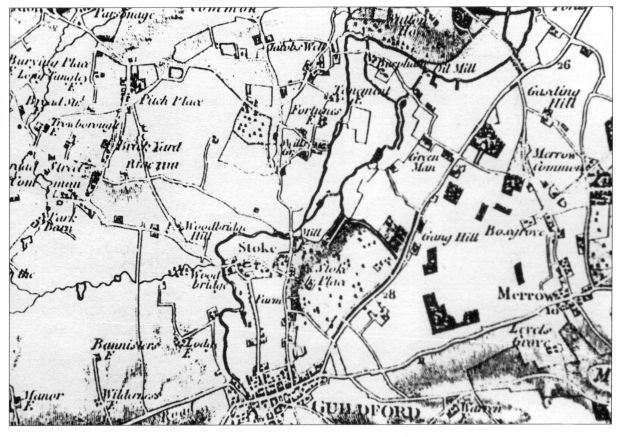

45   O.S. map of 1816, showing Stoke Place

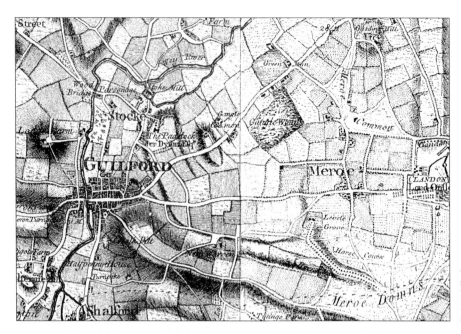

46 Rocque map of 1768 showing the Paddock belonging to Jer: Dyson Esq. and Gangle Wood and Gangle Common.

is found not only on the Senex map of 1729 but also on the Ichnography of Guildford in 1739 (N.E. in the Foxenden area). Perhaps Margaret, widow of Nicholas Turner, who died in 1734 and was buried in the vault where their son subsequently joined them, kept the estate going after the death of her husband. Jonathan, who was responsible for the running of the estate for at least thirteen years (1734-47) had some advice for his younger brother, Nicholas (the second), when he drew up his will just before his death. He urged Nicholas 'to marry some woman suitable to him in family and fortune as soon as may be and make my house at Stoke wherein I now dwell his chief place of residence in the county'.[5] Jonathan Harris obviously had a house of which he felt proud.

It looked at first as if his desire to found a country seat might be realised by his younger brother. Nicholas, described as 'an eloquent poet and scholar', married Anne Towers of Petworth, a woman 'of exquisite beauty', and they settled down in Stoke, where they had three children. This happy rural existence ended when Mrs. Turner died in childbirth in 1753. Her husband, 'distraught with grief',[6] left Stoke and travelled, leaving the children in the care of an aunt, and his brother's hopes of founding a county seat at Stoke were finally disappointed when Nicholas sold the property in 1761.

A Famous Authoress

His eldest daughter, Charlotte, who was born in 1749 and was christened at Stoke Church, spent her childhood at Stoke Park where she is said to have 'fallen in love with nature'. In 1764 her father married again and her aunt persuaded her to marry Benjamin Smith, one of her father's associates in a merchant company trading with the West Indies. She was only 15 years old and was forced by her father-in-law to live in London, over his business premises. Her husband turned out to be an irresponsible spendthrift and in 1782 was imprisoned for debt. His wife shared his seven-month incarceration. She once expressed to a friend a desire that her husband should find rational employment. The friend suggested his enthusiasm might be turned towards religion. Charlotte replied: 'For Heaven's sake do not put it into his head to take to religion for, if he does, he will instantly begin by building a cathedral.'

In 1784 she published a book of poems at her own expense. This was very popular and she decided to turn to writing as the only available way to make money to support her family—she now had 10 children. For a time the family lived in a dilapidated château near Dieppe where Charlotte translated Prévost's *Manon Lescaut*. They then moved to Woolbeding House near Midhurst, and in 1787, now with 12 children, she separated from her husband and turned to writing novels. In 1788 her first novel *Emmeline* or *The Orphans of the Castle* was published in four volumes. This was much admired by Sir Walter Scott. Mrs. Seward thought that the characters of Mr. and Mrs. Stafford were drawn from Mrs. Smith and her husband. *Emmeline* was followed by *Ethelinda* or *The Recluse of the Lake*, by *Celestina* in four volumes, *Desmond* in three volumes and, in 1793, *The Old Manor House* in four volumes, considered by Scott to be her best work. In 1794 she wrote *The Wanderings of Warwick*. In 1795 she turned from novels to *Rural Walks* and *Rambles Farther* and then to natural history and history. A friend wrote: 'Charlotte is writing more volumes … for immediate subsistence; one of the daughters made an imprudent marriage and returned to her mother not worth a shilling and with three young children.' Charlotte's industry was incredible. She published 24 works in 59 volumes and managed to support her family—children, grandchildren and ex-husband—for 22 years. She moved around a good deal, to Brighton, Bath, Oxford, Hastings, Tunbridge Wells, finally to Elstead and then Tilford, where she died on 28 October 1806 aged 57. She

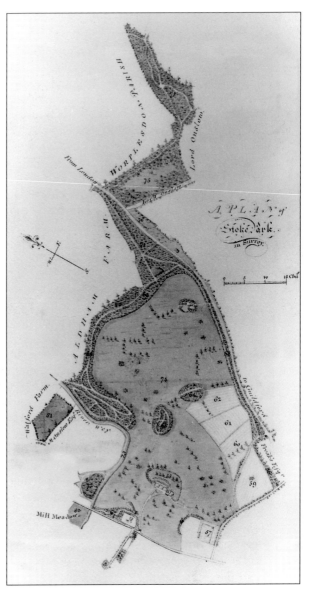

47 Stoke Park from the estate book of 1812

was buried in Stoke Church near her mother Anne and other members of her family. There is a memorial to her high up on the north wall of the chancel. Of her 12 children, eight survived her. Her best loved daughter, Anna Augusta, died in 1795, and her youngest son, George Augustus, lieutenant in the 16th Foot, died in Surinam, five weeks before his mother. Another son, Lionel, became a distinguished soldier. Charlotte was not strong and the fact that so many relied on her for 'immediate subsistence' meant she had to drive herself to continuous output. Today her books and her reputation have completely disappeared, but in her lifetime she was immensely popular. Wordsworth and Coleridge greatly admired her poetry but Sir

Walter Scott considered her novels to be superior. The article on Charlotte Smith in the *Dictionary of National Biography* suggests that while her novels were good on character, they were deficient in plot.[7] Her great strength was her good English style. It is said that whenever Lord Erskine had an important speech to make in the courts he used to read Charlotte Smith in order to catch her 'grace of composition'.[8]

Charlotte must have loved her childhood in Stoke because, although she never lived there after the age of 15, she wanted to be buried there. Her father Nicholas, driven abroad by grief over his wife's death, sold the manor of Stoke to Jeremiah Dyson in 1761, though he appears to have retained some property at Woodbridge (see Chapter Seven).

The Westminster Connection

Dyson was a friend of Speaker Arthur Onslow, which perhaps led Jeremiah to buy a property not far from Clandon. In 1748 he became principal clerk of the House of Commons and made himself master of Commons procedure. He resigned the clerkship in 1762 and became M.P. first of all for Yarmouth (Isle of Wight), then Weymouth in 1768 and Horsham in 1774. In the same year he became Lord of the Treasury and Cofferer of the Royal Household.

He seems to have enjoyed his political life. He was jocularly said to know the journals of the Commons by heart, and intervened so often and so knowledgeably in Commons affairs that in 1769 Colonel Barré provoked general laughter by remarking 'The Hon. Gentleman Mr. Dyson has the devil of a time of it—"Mungo here, Mungo there, Mungo everywhere"', Mungo being a character in a comic opera by Bickerstaffe. The name stuck. 'Mungo' continued to be active in politics and spent his leisure time at Stoke, greatly enjoying 'the air, exercise and idleness'. In 1774 he had a stroke in London and died two years later at Stoke, leaving his son Jeremiah a minor.[9] Later that son placed a memorial on the north wall of Stoughton Chapel where it can still be seen (see Chapter Two).

In 1780 Jeremiah II, now of age, sold the property to George Vansittart, who had been in India and had served on the Bengal Council. There he must have met William Aldersey, who had been on the same Council and who in 1781 bought Stoke Park from George Vansittart.

William Aldersey was born in 1736 and served in the East India Company in Madras. He was sent by Clive to reform the Company's administration in Bengal. In 1772 he became Warren Hastings' deputy in Calcutta and Acting Governor in his absence. Both Clive and Warren Hastings must have thought highly of him, and Richard Wenger in his article in the *Surrey Advertiser* on 16 May 1981 says that, 'Hastings valued his support and "cherished" his friendship'. In 1775 he married Harriet Yorke in Calcutta. Altogether, he spent 25 years in India, and sailed home with his wife and their friend Nathaniel Halhead, Hastings' orientalist, in 1779.

The property which he took over in 1781 is described by Manning and Bray as 'only a Paddock of a few acres adjoining the house',[10] and on Rocque's map of Surrey (1768) 'the Paddock' is the name given to the property. Writing in 1801, Russell says: 'At a small distance south east of Stoke Church is the Paddock, late the seat of William Aldersey. It is a white house surrounded by a pleasant park which is bound on the north by the River Wey and skirted on the south east against the Kingston Road with fine shrubberies.' Where the name Paddock came from is not clear, but it obviously stuck for some time. However, before his death in 1800, Aldersey had greatly enlarged and improved his newly acquired estate, showing the same energy and skill that he had apparently applied to his work in India.

His first achievement has already been described (see Chapter Four). It was to open up the road leading north from Guildford to Woking and Chertsey by shortening and straightening Stoke Road, so that traffic no longer had to make its way down the 'bad, hollow road' to the east of the church but ran straight to a new bridge along an embankment to the west of the church.

This was a great improvement for the traveller. It also enhanced the position of Stoke Park, which now appeared to have the church within its boundaries. At the same time he bought Stoke Paper Mill and Stoke Corn Mill.[11] The new road greatly helped the mills' commerce, and the new management of the river meant increased flow of water to the mills and also 'the embellishment of his pleasure grounds'.[12]

Aldersey also bought, from Lord Onslow, the demesne lands of Stoughton and became Lord of the Manors of both Stoke and Stoughton. He did much to enlarge his property by buying up neighbouring farms, for example Ganghill Farm, again from Lord Onslow, and Oldham (or Aldham) Farm, for which he paid £3,920, with timber at £87 13s. 0d.[13]

The only surviving Court Book provides an interesting example of Aldersey's approach to his property. In it there is a reference to an Act of Parliament passed in 1789. This was 'an Act for enclosing by the mutual consent of the Lord and tenants part of any commons for the purpose of planting and preserving trees for Timber and Underwood and for the more effectually preventing the unlawful destruction of trees'. This was fol-lowed by a similar act in 1791 and the commons mentioned are Ganghill Common, New Pond, Tilehouse Farm and Woodbridge Hill. After Aldersey's death, at Nathaniel Hillier's first Court Baron in 1803, there is a reminder: 'Be it re-membered that on 23rd of December 1793 there was general agreement by those who have right of common pasture in the wastelands or grounds of the said manor that William Aldersey should enclose this land.'[14] The fact that Aldersey's con-servation measures had to be reiterated by Nathaniel Hillier suggests that those who had given up rights in the commons and wasteland during Aldersey's life were having second thoughts after his death. But the Acts of Parlia-ment of 1789 and 1791 were sufficient to safe-guard the trees of Stoke Park, a feature preserved by William Aldersey's efforts and one which would later receive general acclaim. However, at the time the enforced enclosure of common land was very unpopular.

As far as the house was concerned, it is probable that the Turners began the process of building it but, in view of the energy shown by Aldersey in developing his property, it seems likely that 'he extended it and was responsible for the major part of the 18th century work' at Stoke Park Mansion. John Baker, in the *Surrey Advertiser* of January 1976, writes of an Adamesque frieze in the first and second floor rooms at the curved end, and a very good

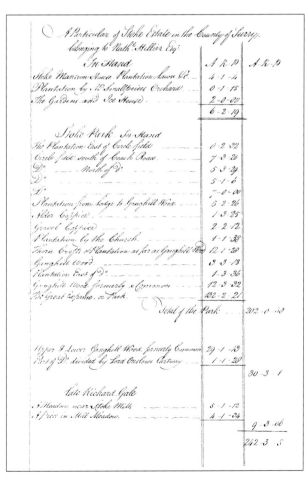

48 A Particular of Stoke Estate belonging to Nathaniel Hillier

49   Rose garden in Stoke Park

fireplace, as well as 'a gem of small stair', but all this went in the demolition of 1977.

William Aldersey was also interested in music, was a subscriber to *A General History of Music* written by Dr. Burney, the King's Musician (and father of Fanny Burney), and in 1785 he gave a three manual organ to the church. Halhead, who returned from India with the Alderseys and often visited them, wrote of 'the morning trio', which seems likely to have been of the musical kind as he also dedicated several poems to 'the musical Alderseys'.[15]

Richard Wenger mentions two other visitors to Stoke Park. One was Aldersey's cousin, Captain Thomas Forrest, a sailor who 'made a voyage of exploration to New Guinea and the Moluccas'. He published his journal in 1780 and dedicated an engraving in the book to 'his amiable cousin'.

Mr. Wenger also mentions Quentin Crawford, who served under Aldersey in Madras. He was involved in attempts to save the French Royal Family during the Revolution. His mother and one of her granddaughters are commemorated in Stoke Church.

Stoke Park was undoubtedly a place of resort for those who had been involved in the administration of India, and with its woods and terraces and its banks sloping down to the River Wey, it provided a perfect rural retreat, a retreat which Aldersey was reluctant to leave. In 1784 he became High Sheriff of the County, and began canvassing as prospective M.P. for Guildford in 1789, but decided against political life and withdrew to Stoke before the election.

After Aldersey's death Halhead dedicated a poem to Mrs. Aldersey recalling his visits in utopian terms:

> O Stoke! Thy lawns, thy watermill, thy trees,
> The cordial owner and the welcom'd guest,
> The splendid neatness and the rural ease,
> The ride, the walk, the philosophic page,
> The morning trio and gay converse sweet,
> To cheer the spirits or the thoughts engage,
> Or give the pulse of health a steadied beat.

Aldersey was 64 years old when he died on 30 May 1800, having carved out a successful career in India and then made Stoke a perfect place for his retirement. His wife lived until 1846 having married again, 15 years after William's death. In addition to endowing the organ given by her husband, she raised to his memory the worthiest monument in her power by the best-known sculptor of the time, John Flaxman R.A.: a grieving woman by an urn. It stands against the north wall of Stoke Church and the subscription says:

This Monument was erected by Harriet Aldersey in grateful remembrance of the most affectionate of Husbands William Aldersey, Esq. of Stoke Park, a Place formed by his taste, enlivened by his cheerfulness, made happy by his bounty and better by his example.

Their only child died in infancy and Mrs. Aldersey sold Stoke Park along with the lordship of the manor to Nathaniel Hillier in 1801.

The Hilliers were a nonconformist family, and although they were members of the Mercers' Company they had branched out into printing and book-selling. Nathaniel, the father, had a valuable collection of prints and drawings. The son who bought Stoke Park had been born in 1740 and was therefore over 60 when he moved to Stoke, but he was not idle. He followed the example of William Aldersey and planted many trees on his estate; to quote Richard Wenger again, 'years later Stoke Park was described as "adorned with some of the most magnificent timber in the country"'. He also collected fragments of 15th and 16th-century glass which were made up into a window in the east wall of the Stoughton Chapel. At Clandon there are portraits of Nathaniel Hillier and his wife,

50 Stoke Park, Guildford. 'The Thirty Acres' (Hockey)

incorporating views of the park and the church. He was meticulous in recording the extent of his property.[16] He inherited from his predecessor the question of responsibility for the repair and upkeep of Stoke bridges, and although at first the magistrates concluded that he had full responsibility, he proposed a solution which was adopted and after his death the County took over (see Chapter 5).

He also organised new arrangements for the manorial courts. They were to meet at Watford Farm, 'the scite of the manors of Stoughton and Stoke' (see Chapter 7). He lived to enjoy his estate for nine years, dying in 1810 at the age of 70. He and his wife were both buried in St Giles, Camberwell, but they have a memorial tablet in Stoke Church.

51 Stoke Park, a riding lesson

52   Stoke Park football team, 1922-3

They had two daughters. He settled Stoke Park on his elder daughter, Harriet, who married Colonel James Bogle Delap. It became the Delaps' home for 50 years, Harriet surviving her husband as a childless widow by many years. Nathaniel had arranged that if she had no children it was to pass to her sister Susannah, who was a considerable artist and who married Thomas Cranley Onslow who, before his marriage in 1812, had distinguished himself in the Peninsular War. He was the younger brother of the 3rd Earl of Onslow, whose only son died in 1852. In 1853 William Hillier was born to the son of Susannah (née Hillier) and Thomas Cranley Onslow, which accounts for the inclusion of Hillier in his name, and he became the heir of the Onslow Estate and of Stoke Park when he succeeded to the title in 1870.

53   Entrance to Stoke Park House when it was a school

The 4th Earl of Onslow found a very dilapidated Clandon estate as his great-uncle had not lived there for many years and had allowed everything to fall into ruin. The 17-year-old inheritor had so much to do to rescue Clandon that he decided to sell the Stoke part of his inheritance. From 1862-9 Stoke Park was leased to Charles Hulse.[16]

54 South-east view of the school

In 1879 he sold the lordship of the manor and the mansion with 109 acres to James Smith Budgett of Ealing Park for £24,000.[17] He was head of the firm of James Budgett and Son Ltd., sugar brokers and merchants of Laurence Pountney Lane E.C. He retired to Stoke at the age of 55 and made some alterations to the house (designated by John Baker as 'unfortunate remodelling'). He also built Stoke Lodge in 1881, reminiscent of the work of Norman Shaw, and Stoke Model Farm opening on to Nightingale Road, at that time called the New Road. He played a part in local affairs, being on the Board of Management of the Royal Surrey County Hospital from 1881 onwards, and a member of Guildford and Woking Men's Institute of which he was elected President in 1892. He presented a book of his Travel Sketches to the Institute and there is a plaque in the wall of the Institute which mentions his presidency.

He was a staunch Wesleyan but towards the end of his life he went to services in Stoke Parish Church. There is a memorial window there to his daughter-in-law Anne, his son Richard's wife, who died in 1888 at the age of 28. James added 83 acres to Stoke Park in the Burchatt's Farm and Thorneycroft area before his death in 1906 aged 82. His widow continued to live at Stoke until her death in 1912. From 1913-15 the house appears as vacant in the Directories, but in 1916 Richard returned to live there until he died in 1919. His successor, Herbert Maitland

55 Stoke Park *c*.1865, before the 'improvements' introduced by James Budgett

Budgett of Idol Lane in the City of London, never lived at Stoke Park and in 1922 leased it to C.E. Lewis of Shere to be used as a 'high class boarding school for boys'. Guildford Museum has numerous photographs and a prospectus of Stoke Park Preparatory School. It was run by Mr. and Mrs. Lewis and Mrs. Lewis continued after her husband's death.

In 1925 H.M. Budgett agreed to sell to Guildford Corporation the whole of the Stoke Park estate, and when the school closed in 1935 the Corporation leased the Mansion House to the County Council to be used as a Technical College. John Baker and many others opposed the destruction of Stoke Park Mansion House but its demolition nevertheless took place in November 1977. We must be grateful that the park itself has survived. Created by the lords of the manor of Stoke, it is an invaluable green lung for north-east Guildford, and escaped becoming the site of a new County Hall, in the area which the Spectrum Leisure Centre now occupies to the north of the by-pass.

The Borough's decision to acquire Stoke Park may have been partly motivated by the need to provide a by-pass for traffic. The only road through Guildford was the High Street and the increase in traffic made some sort of by-pass essential. Nine acres of the 185 acres sold by Mr. Budgett were to be taken up by a new arterial road. Without this road and the by-pass of the 1980s, Guildford's traffic problems would have been insoluble. Moreover, the County made a point of preserving the park. E.R. Chamberlin points out that, while the road was still being built, the Surrey County Council Act of 1931 limited access and house building so that ribbon development was avoided and the first by-pass runs through pleasant parkland.[18] It was opened in July 1934.

A Famous Lido

While the road-work was going on another project was undertaken in another corner of Stoke Park. This was the building of the Lido in circumstances which attracted national attention. The Great Depression of the 1930s led to levels of unemployment hitherto unknown, and many men 'got on their bikes', as a later generation was exhorted to do, in search of work. The news of the building of the Guildford by-pass attracted unemployed from all over the country, more than could find work at the site. At any rate, by the end of 1932 Guildford had 657 unemployed men and the Mayor of Guildford announced a scheme which was adopted by the Borough Council. It established the Mayor's Work Fund, to which the Council contributed £3,000 and the public—at first from Guildford but then from further afield—£7,720, by the end of the scheme in June 1933. William Harvey believed that 'our unemployed need work not charity', and his aim was to employ men on various projects under the direct control of the Council and, of the many projects embarked on, the single most important one was the open air swimming pool set in 4½ acres of landscaped grounds, in Stoke Park, near Stoke Church. In fact almost the only objection raised was by the rector of Stoke who thought that noise from the Lido might disturb the church. In spite of this the work went ahead and provided employment for 120 men for nearly six months. Two hundred and twenty local authorities wrote for details of the Mayor's Work Fund and the idea was adopted in 27 other areas. The opening ceremony was reported worldwide, and William Harvey took the first dive into this new amenity in Stoke Park on 21 June 1933.[19]

Other amenities were developed in Stoke Park as the Judges postcard of the Rose Garden shows.

Six

Boundaries, Courts and Census Lists

Quarrels over Boundaries

The boundaries of the borough of Guildford had always enclosed a comparatively small area to include, to the west only the High Street running down to the town mills and land at the foot of the Mount; to the north, the north town ditch or Lower Backside, later North Street; and to the south Upper Backside, now Sydenham Road. The eastern boundary only just included the Royal Grammar School. Beyond that circumscribed area lay the manor of Stoke. Russell's *History and Antiquities of Guildford* and the Ichnography of 1739 both show how closely the ancient manor hugged Guildford on the north and east, conscious perhaps that it had at least as long a history behind it as Guildford. Perhaps it was this that made Stoke an awkward neighbour, determined not to surrender any of its rights to the much more populous borough next door.

There are several recorded examples of this determination and there may well have been many more. In 1626, the Mayor and Approved Men of Guildford requested a renewal of the town's charters with the important addition of jurisdiction over Stoke above Bars (Upper High Street) and Stoke Lane (Chertsey Street). Their reason for requesting this extension of power was that those places were 'full of disorderly persons, and malefactors do daily increase', and the Mayor and Approved Men accounted for this as follows:

> because the Constable and Tything man of Stoke within which manor and Leet of Stoke those places be ... have been chosen of late out of those liberties ... so that neither constable nor tythingman is resident whereby malefactors might the more speedily be apprehended and warrants more speedily executed.[1]

The Lost Charter

This request seemed reasonable to Charles I and in 1627 he confirmed existing privileges to Guildford and extended the borough boundaries to include Stoke above Bars and Stoke Lane. To the people of Stoke, however, this seemed extremely unreasonable, especially taking into account the hole and corner way in which it was done. They therefore immediately petitioned the King:

> The humble petition of the inhabitants of the parish of Stoke neere Guildford ... who humbly show that the said inhabitants have always maintained a watch for your Majesty and your royal predecessors ... and on all occasions at Stoke Cross and Lanes near Stoke Church and likewise at ye Beacon. But now they are not able to perform the said Watch, being but a third part of the said parish: for the other two parts called Stoke above Barre and Stoke Lane are included in the new Charter of Guildford in Anno 1626 by an unreasonable, fraudulent petition to your Majesty from the good men of the towne of Guildford. John Champion, towne Clearke, being an agent for them hath inserted into the said Charter more than in the said petition is specified all which was done without the knowledge or consent of the said inhabitants.' [Note: Was the Beacon the same as for Guildford (on the Hog's Back) or was it a different one (as seems likely), perhaps on Browning's Down?]

The people of Stoke go on to ask the King 'out of your gracious goodness to referre the examination to the right Hon. Sir George Moore' and other knights of the shire. This the King did from his Court at Whitehall on 19 February 1628. The people of Stoke had their say before the Committee: 'since the memory of man the parishioners of Stoke have always maintained watch and ward … at Stoke', and they protested most strongly against 'laying the whole service upon the remaining third part' (of the population) 'to the burden, separation, trouble and great grief of all the said inhabitants', and finally they pointed out that maintaining the highways would also fall upon the unfortunate 'third parte' and this was not to be borne since 'such ways are so many that in length they contain eight miles at the least …'. One can see what they meant: Stoke above Barre and Stoke Lane were the most populated parts of the parish and local duties would fall most heavily on the least populated. But perhaps they protested too much. The knights of the shire left control of the two areas with Guildford, and as watch and ward entailed so many duties they proposed that the Mayor and five Approved Men should be made responsible for supervising the maintenance of law and order in those areas.[2]

Armed with their new charter, the Mayor and Approved Men then proceeded to tidy up the disputed areas. In 1627 they issued 'an order concerning Stoke above Barr and Stoke Lanes next joining to the Towne with many good branches for the good governing thereof'. These included 'Four persons to be yearly chosen in Stoke above Barr to make presentment every three weeks',[3] i.e. report any wrongdoers. Later, 'It is also ordered that no person owning … any habitation in Guildford or places adjoining or added to the government of this towne do let any house, shop or room to a forryner.'[4] Thus Guildford set about establishing order in those areas of Stoke which the King had included in the Charter of 1627.

The strange thing is that this Charter apparently never took effect. The original was lost and the existence of the Charter forgotten until it was rediscovered in the 19th century by the compiler of a set of translations of the Guildford charters. The parishioners of Stoke certainly never reminded Guildford of the arrangements laid down in 1627, so that until the Municipal Corporations Act of 1835 Guildford was governed under the Charter of Charles I without extensions into Stoke.

There were other disputes between the manor and the borough. For instance, at a Court Leet of the manor of Stoke on 17 April 1681 it was presented that

> the Mayor of Guildford then being, had pulled down a certain Bar in Stoke above Barr within the jurisdiction of this Leet which was an ancient boundary between the Parish of Stoke and the Town of Guildford, whereupon the mayor of Guildford aforesaid was oftentimes commanded to build up the Bar under divers penalties but he wholly refused. Therefore he was further commanded to build up the Bar … before the Feast of St John Baptist next following under penalty of ten shillings.[5]

Unfortunately there do not appear to be any documents which tell us the result of this particular encounter.

The only one of the Stoke Court Books which survive, records the appointment of William Joseph as Constable and throws light on the development of Stoke Park under William Aldersey. It also shows that Stoke took a fairly relaxed attitude to its manorial duties by the end of the 18th century. The Court Baron met infrequently, about every seven years. The Court Leet of 1803 recorded of Stoke above Barr and Stoke below Barr, 'It appeared that no Tithingman had been chosen there for many years.' John Day was duly appointed Tithingman for those districts. Unfortunately, at the Court Leet of 1811, 'John Day, Tithingman, being called, the Court are informed he is dead'.[6] The same applied to William Taylor, Aletaster. However, Stoke still had its Constable, William Joseph, who also took on the job of Pounder. It looks as if the local administration depended almost entirely on William Joseph at the beginning of the 19th century!

Court Days at Watford

However, Nathaniel Hillier made a new arrangement for the meeting place of the manorial courts. In 1806 he let Watford Farm to George Smallpeice of Stoke, gent., with the right to repair and rebuild Watford Farm House. The provision of glass and lead for windows was to be the responsibility of Nathaniel Hillier, while George would provide the thatch. At the same time George was to be the Bailiff of the Manor of Stoke and Stoughton, to collect rents and provide dinner on Court Days at Watford Farm, 'said to be the scite of the Manors of Stoughton and Stoke'.[7] Watford was certainly an old site. There are documents showing that George Parvis, yeoman, brother of John Parvis of Unstead, lived at Watford in Stoke from 1569 onwards.[8] By 1587 he had become 'Geo. Parvish of Watford, Stoke, gent.' with a mansion called Watford. What happened to the mansion so clearly marked on Senex's map of 1729 and described in detail in Dyson's abstract of title (see Chapter Four) is not clear, but a large farmhouse survived and was worth doing up in 1806 and making into the headquarters of the manorial courts, some of which are recorded in the surviving Court Book. So Watford Farm followed Warren Farm and Court Close as the meeting place of Stoke's manorial courts.

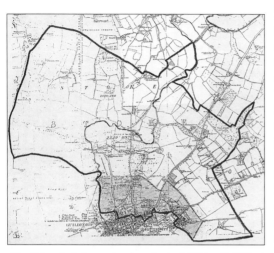

56   The shaded area became Stoke Within Guildford under the Municipal Corporation Act of 1835.

The life of these courts, however, was drawing to a close. In 1835 the Municipal Corporations Act followed the Great Reform Act of 1832 and made necessary some attempt to tidy up the administration of municipal boroughs. As far as Stoke was concerned, this meant losing all the border area nearest to the borough of Guildford. This was to be called Stoke Within (Guildford), and the rest of the ancient manor retained its name of Stoke Next Guildford. Thus two centuries after the attempt to include Stoke above Bars and Stoke Lanes within the borough boundaries, Guildford at last succeeded.

It is extraordinary that this had not happened before and that this arrangement of Stoke Within and Stoke-next-Guildford continued to operate until 1904. In that year the Guildford Borough Extension Order was passed amid much debate. That part which had been known as Stoke Within was renamed Christchurch Ward and the rest of Stoke gave up the centuries-old 'next-Guildford' label and was incorporated into the borough of Guildford. This was not done without a great deal of discussion, the vicar of Emmanuel Church, Stoughton being one of those in favour of the change: 'We should throw ourselves heartily into the wider life of "Greater Guildford" and send from our midst representatives to the Corporation who will care for our interests and for those of the whole area'.[9] In spite of the old names being officially dropped, they continued in general use for many years. On a sale map of 1912 the boundaries of both Stoke-next-Guildford and Stoke Within are clearly shown. After the 1914-18 War Stoke, although now part of Guildford, erected its own war memorial.

The Census in Stoke

There was one set of people however who welcomed the disappearance of Stoke, at any rate from an administrative point of view. These were the people responsible for drawing up the Census Lists. Time after time they start with a definition of the boundaries between the Parish of Stoke and the Borough of Guildford. In 1841 they record the boundaries as follows:

Superintendent Registrar's District _Guildford_ Enumeration District, No. _2 R S H_ '23

Registrar's Sub-District _Guildford_ Name of Enumerator, Mr. _William Smart_

DESCRIPTION OF ENUMERATION DISTRICT.

[This description is to be written in by the Enumerator from the Copy supplied to him by the Registrar. Any explanatory notes or observations calculated to make the description clearer or more complete, may be added by the Enumerator].

All that part of the Parish of Stoke next Guildford including Chertsey Street, with Stoke Road, and Courts and Alleys on both sides down to the New Road — New Road, Quills' Farm, King's Road, Drummond Road, Dapdune Woodbridge Road from — Dapdune to North Street, including Hack's Row and Gas Works — Grafham Road & Frog Lane, including Sea Dale House, all in the Borough of Guildford.

57 The enumerators struggle to define Guildford/Stoke boundaries in 1861: 'all in the Borough of Guildford'

58 The enumerators list those places 'not included in the borough of Guildford'

Superintendent Registrar's District _Guildford_ Enumeration District, No. _1 E_

Registrar's Sub-District _Guildford_ Name of Enumerator, Mr. _John Pearce_ 1-2

DESCRIPTION OF ENUMERATION DISTRICT.

[This description is to be written in by the Enumerator from the Copy supplied to him by the Registrar. Any explanatory notes or observations calculated to make the description clearer or more complete, may be added by the Enumerator].

No. 1 E.
Parish of Stoke next Guildford

All that part of the Parish of Stoke next Guildford not included in the Borough of Guildford including new Barn, Warren Farm & Cottages, 4 houses at the top of Cowshide, Watford Farm, Pit Farm, Hendricks Farm & Cottages, Stoke Park Lodge, Box Grove road, Brick Kilns, Gunghill Farm, Stoke Park Villa, Stoke Park & Gardeners Cottage, Parsonage, Stoke Corn & Paper Mills, Stoke Lock, Stoke Hill Lodge, Bell Road, Slyfield Green & the houses between there & Stoke Hill Malt house, Stoke Hill Farm, Stoughton & Lodges, Tile house Farm, Woodbridge Hill, Woodbridge house and Cottages, and Josephs Lane.

All that part of the Parish of Stoke having for its boundary the road leading from Guildford to Woodbridge on the west, Joseph's Lane on the north and Stoke Lane with the road leading from Stoke Lane to Stoke Bridges on the east, including the Leas, Dapdune, Stoke Parsonage and Stoke Lane exclusive of the Lunatic Asylum.

In 1861 they are still at it, as the two descriptions of the Enumeration Districts show: that part not included and that part included in the Borough of Guildford.[10] In 1933 there was a further extension of Borough boundaries and squabbles over them became a thing of the past.

The Ancient Korporation of Stoke

Although disputes became a thing of the past, Stoke itself derived some amusement, as Guildford must also have done, from the formation of the Ancient Korporation of Stoke, founded about 1878, which met every week at the *Prince of Wales Hotel* (opposite the old Cattle Market in Woodbridge Road) to discuss decisions made by Guildford Borough Council. 'Our reports appeared in the *West Surrey Times*, in Old English.' The aim was to poke fun in a light-hearted way at the serious business of local government and 'to pull the legs' of the Borough Councillors. The Korporation contained every possible ancient official and some fairly impossible ones:

59   The parish of Stoke raised its own war memorial although Stoke had disappeared administratively

Ye mayore, four Eldermen (in Light Blue), 12 Kouncillors, Mace Bearer, Tipstaff, Sword Bearer, Inspector of Nuisances and Beer Tester. 'On the opening of the new Onslow Bridge in 1882 the Korporation of Ye Provynce of Stoke erected an arch and Ye Ancient Korporation of Ye Provynce of Stoke assembled in their robes and were given a hearty welcome.' On another occasion 'Ye Mayore and Korporation' went down the River Wey in a barge and boats to claim their rights over the river, and on arrival at the Row Barge 'Ye Beer Taster and Inspector were sent to sample the drink (Crooke's pure malt and hops beer) which was pronounced satisfactory and consumed by all'.[11]

An idiotic game, but amusing, and turning an ancient rivalry into an enjoyable and peaceful pastime.

· Ye · Antiente ·

Korporatione of ye Provynce of Stoke.

"To hold as t'were ye mirror up to nature."—Shakespeare.
Hamlet, Act iii., Scene ii.

Oyez! Oyez! Oyez!

Let it bee knowne *to alle ye goode & trvstye*

Burgeſſes of this Antiente Korporatione

That ye Maſtere Mayore dothe greete you ryghte heartilie aftere youre holy-dai & nowe dothe calle upon eache & everie of you ryghte faithfullie to come & discharge youre duties inne Kouncille aſſembled inne ye Royale Chambere on ye eveninge of Thurſdaye ye XXXth dai of Septembere MDCCCLXXX atte ye ſtrikinge of VIII of ye clocke for divers buſineſſe

60 A summons to the Burgesses of Stoke, 1880

Seven

Woodbridge

More Bridge Problems

In the *Book of Surrey Placenames*, Wodebrigge appears early, though not as early as Stoke. According to the *Victoria County History* it was held by the Poyle family, and the earliest tenant seems to have been Thomas de Woodbridge, who held it in 1264 or thereabouts. In 1272 'La Wodebrigge' appears in the Assize Rolls and a 'pons de Wodebrigge' in 1356. In 1324 it was described as a messuage and five acres of land in Stoke and its connection with Stoke continued. Manning and Bray report that in the reign of Richard II (1377-99) the Inquest found that the bridge at this place ought to be repaired by the people of the neighbourhood and their charitable contributions and not by the Bishop of London as Lord of the Manor.[1] In Appendix XXXVIII Manning and Bray pursue the problem of the bridge:

> In 1694/5 doubts were entertained whether the county was liable and a Rate having been made, the inhabitants … objected to the payment and on a fair trial they were acquitted and the Rate returned. In 1719 an order was made at the Midsummer Sessions for repairing that part of the bridge which belonged to the County. In 1735 the County was indicted and a similar order made.

Bridge repairing was expensive and both sides manoeuvred to avoid responsibility. In 1745 a contract was made for repair and the whole business was brought to a successful conclusion when, in 1766, 'the present excellent causeway was made by the County … where there used to be a very bad, wet way, in frosts impassable'.

Woodbridge and Stoke Bridges were near neighbours and their problems were similar. The bad, wet, hollow ways had to be eliminated but the County took responsibility only after centuries of avoidance.

Two Houses at Woodbridge

Joseph's Lane ran west towards the river. To the south lay two properties. Nearest the river with lawns running down to the water stood a house which on the Tithe Award Map is called Woodbridge House. East of this property, to the east of Woodbridge Road, stood another house labelled 'Mansion Garden Lawn'. On the 1912 6in. O.S. map what had been Woodbridge House in 1841 is Woodbridge Park, while the 'mansion' of 1841 is called Woodbridge House. Both of them have long disappeared so perhaps it does not matter that different houses were known by the same name at different times. However, when Manning and Bray, writing in 1804, say that 'Woodbridge House was the property of Nicholas Turner Esq., not sold by him with the principal estate and continued his residence after he had quitted the great House',[2] they must mean the estate nearer the river later known as Woodbridge Park. So it would seem that Nicholas Turner, when he sold Stoke Park to Jeremiah Dyson after his wife's death, did not spend all his time abroad but kept a *pied à terre* at Woodbridge, and was probably responsible for starting the building which may have been known at first as Woodbridge Cottage and only later as Woodbridge House and then Woodbridge Park.

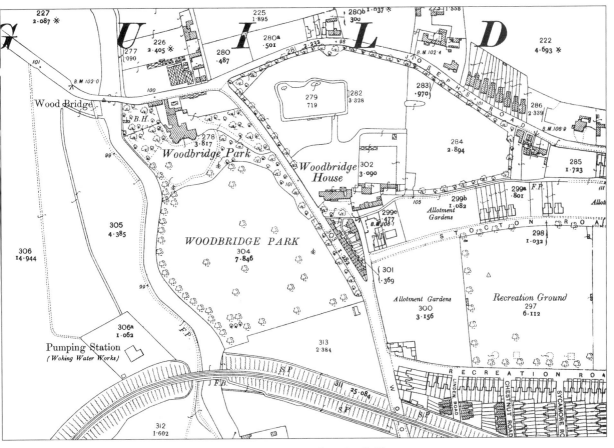

61 Map of 1912 showing the Woodbridge estates

The Mangles

The family which put Woodbridge on the map and extended knowledge of its name to the Antipodes was the Mangles family. The Mangles brothers, James and John, were the sons of a 'ship chandler at Wapping'. They did well and built up a successful shipping firm which traded with the East Indies and Australia. The fleet included the *Mangles*, the *Guildford* and the *Surrey*. In 1791 James married Mary Hughes at Worplesdon, and soon after established himself at Woodbridge. With his brother he founded the Mangles Bank which is listed in Russell's Almanack of 1842 as Mangles Bros., 49 High Street, West Surrey Bank. He became High Sheriff of the County in 1807 and from 1831-7 he was M.P. for Guildford in the Whig interest. In 1837, the election was a three-cornered affair which James Mangles lost in spite of his lively poster appeal to the electors

62 James Mangles died in 1838. This lithograph of Woodbridge Cottage was probably printed before that

63 This view from Eric Hunter's collection shows how James Mangles' 'Cottage' was extended

of Guildford. More on elections can be found in Shirley Corke's *Guildford: a pictorial history*, nos. 112-5. From the same source we learn that in 1837, aged 74, Mangles was successfully operated on for a cataract. In 1834 he was one of the founders of the Guildford Institute, and he died in 1838. He had a large family of 12 children, at least two of whom had notable careers.

Ross Donnelly Mangles (1801-77) was educated at Eton and at the East India Company college at Haileybury. In 1819 he entered the Bengal Civil Service, rose in the ranks and held numerous offices. In 1833 he became magistrate and collector of customs and land revenues at Chittagong and Agra. In 1835 he held the important post of Secretary to the Government of Bengal, a position he held with great effect until his final return to England in 1839; how effectively is shown by the title bestowed on him by the natives. They always referred to him as Lord Mangles, completely sure he was the equal in title as in everything to his two colleagues, Lord Colvin and Lord Auckland.[3] In 1841 he followed his father by standing in the Liberal interest for Parliament. He was elected and continued to be returned for Guildford until 1858. He also served as the Chairman of the East India Company, and as a member of the Mangles Banking Company. His son, Ross Lewis Mangles, won the Victoria Cross during the Indian Mutiny.

Ellen Mangles

In the large family of 12 children who grew up on the banks of the Wey, Ellen, born in 1807, also had a notable career. Her father James, while organising the Mangles' trade in the east, had met a young naval commander from Scotland, the 15th child of Andrew and Ann Stirling of Lanarkshire. He was born in 1791 into a family with a long tradition of service in the Royal Navy and by the age of 21, in 1812, he had become commander of the *Brazen*. His name was James Stirling. At the end of the Napoleonic wars he managed to avoid retirement on half pay by undertaking the shadowing and protection of ships to the outposts of the empire, including Australia, and it was in this connection that James Mangles met him and they became friends. Mangles invited him to visit Woodbridge when he was on shore leave, and in 1820 James remembered this invitation and, hiring a horse and carriage from Guildford, went out to Woodbridge. As he drove up the drive he had to swerve to avoid hitting a small girl riding two small ponies

with one foot on the back of each, as if practis-
ing to become a circus performer. He learned
from Captain Mangles that this was Ellen, one of
the captain's daughters, then aged 13. After that
James Stirling often visited Woodbridge, particularly after being put on half pay, and in
1823—on Ellen's 16th birthday—they were
married at Stoke Church.

In 1826 he was given command of a new
ship, the *Success*, and sent to form a settlement
in Raffles Bay, Torres Strait, because of French
activity in the Pacific. Stirling pointed out to
Governor Darling that it was the wrong time
of year for this project because the monsoon
was just due to start in that northern region.
Rather than keep Stirling idle in Botany Bay,
Governor Darling decided to send him to report on the west coast of Australia and on
whether the French or the Dutch showed any
signs of having designs on the area. His exploration of the country, as he made his way up
the Swan River, convinced him that an English
settlement should be established. Even at this
early stage he named an inland island 'Guildford' and the land near it on the banks of the
river 'Woodbridge'. On his return he tried to
persuade the authorities of the value of a settlement but they jibbed at the probably excessive
cost. In the end it was agreed that Stirling should
try but that it must be a privately funded enterprise. If investors and settlers could be found,
Stirling could be the new governor but must
take his salary in the form of a land grant. An

64 Both the lithograph and this upright view from Eric
Hunter's collection show how close the house stood to the
river

enormous publicity campaign began—Swan River Mania—and on 9 February 1829 the *Parmelia*,
with about 100 people on board, set sail from Plymouth for the 16-week voyage to found the
Swan River Colony. The *Parmelia*, along with HMS *Sulpher*, arrived off the Western Australian
coast on 31 May and on 18 June 1829 Stirling proclaimed the foundation of the colony. On
12 August Perth was founded.

Western Australia

The settlers who sailed in the *Parmelia* came mainly from Worplesdon and Pirbright. Ellen
Stirling (née Mangles) and her husband sailed with them. She had her small son Andrew with
her and during the voyage gave birth to Frederick Henry. He was later to take command of the
British Navy in Australian waters.

The early days of the new colony were hard and Ellen was only 22 when she arrived at the Swan
River, but from the first she seems to have played an important part in smoothing away opposition
to her husband, providing help for settlers in difficulty and organising the social life of the colony.

In addition she bore 11 children. James took 4,000 acres for his estate. Here he built a house on the banks of the river, modelled on Captain Mangles' house on the Wey, and called it Woodbridge. On a visit to England in 1832 he was knighted, but he continued to administer the colony until the end of 1838. In 1839 he and Ellen returned to Woodbridge in England, but Stirling's career was not yet over. He was put in command first of HMS *Indus*, then HMS *Howe*, and then appointed Commander-in-Chief of China and the East Indies stations from 1854-6. Ellen continued to live at Woodbridge. In 1862 he became a full Admiral, and died at Woodbridge in 1865. Ellen lived until 1874, when she was buried beside her husband in Stoke Churchyard. When the parish of Stoke decided to build a new community centre in 1981, they named it the Stirling Centre after Sir James and Ellen, Lady Stirling, who had founded Woodbridge on the other side of the world.[4]

Woodbridge Cottage?

The Mangles estate is shown clearly on the Tithe Award Map of 1841. James Mangles had died in 1838 and so when the map was drawn up his widow Mary was in possession. She is shown as the owner of land on both sides of the river north of Woodbridge House and the bridge, Bridge Meadow on the left bank, Long Meadow on the right bank, the boat house and yard by the bridge on the left, the garden and forcing house on the right, as well as the barn yard and stable (presumably where Ellen's ponies had lived). A large paddock stretched down as far as Dapdune. On the O.S.6in. map of 1873 Woodbridge Cottage is also marked, but this cannot be the subject of the lithograph by C. Burton, printed by Simonan. The O.S. cottage is not near water but the Simonan etching shows both a pond with boys fishing and a barge with two men aboard on the river. It is titled 'The Seat of James Mangles Esq.'. It has lawns stretching down to the river and it is tempting to conclude that this is the Woodbridge House where the 12 Mangles grew up and which was the model for the Woodbridge estate in Western Australia. The photographs of Woodbridge from Eric Hunter's collection show how the house extended as the family grew and how close it stood to the river which reflected it.

65 David Rose of the *Surrey Advertiser* has very kindly given me permission to include this rare photograph of Woodbridge House. It is taken from the *Surrey Advertiser* book *Images of Guildford*

Eight
Benefactors and Beneficiaries

Stoke Hospital—The Parson Brothers' Gift to Stoke

This beautiful building in Stoke Road was the brainchild of the Parson brothers, William and Henry. Their father had married a widow from Farnham, Mrs. Trimmer, who had children by her first marriage and, by her second marriage, a daughter, Sarah, and two sons, William and Henry. None of these three married and all helped to run the thriving drapery business in Guildford High Street. So prosperous did they become that there were rumours of the discovery of hidden treasure in the cellar to account for their wealth. Sarah worked along with her brothers and was noted both for her sweet disposition and her shrewd business sense. Mr. Philip Palmer, in his privately printed paper on Stoke Hospital and its founders (1916), records an oral tradition concerning Sarah in the shop:

> Two local wags, to put her temper to the test, examined length after length and at last one of them tendered a shilling. 'I will take a shilling's worth of this.' Miss Parson calmly cut a disc from the corner of the cloth selected, the exact size of the shilling, and handed it to him with a serene smile, putting the shilling into the till.'

The brothers retired to a house just outside Guildford, in Stoke. Mr. Baker says that it was called The White House, Mr. Palmer that it was probably The Firs.

With some of the wealth they had accumulated, they decided to build and endow a hospital for six poor widows from Stoke. Before the scheme could be carried out, Henry died on 25 March 1791, aged 62 years.

His brother William went ahead, determined to make the idea of Stoke Hospital a reality. In 1792 he bought:

> Part of field called Barnfield, now in the occupation of Ann Covey … abuts on the high road from Stoke Lane to Stoke Church on the west, on Love Lane on the south and on other parts of the field on east and north.[1]

At first the area measured 140ft. on each side, but in 1794 the hospital was finished and the first six widows took up residence. Mr. Palmer gives their names and also the names of the Trustees who were made responsible for the management of the hospital. The Founder's Statutes are printed in Russell's *History of Antiquities of Guildford*, p.272. They included the provision that the inmates should be known as 'Sisters', that they should attend services at the parish church twice on Sundays and in their own chapel on Wednesdays and Fridays. The front gate was to be opened from 7am to 8pm in the summer and from 8a.m. to 6p.m. in winter. No sister was to be out after the gate was shut. The Sisters were to receive 4s. per week, the matron 5s. and all were to be provided with a broadcloth blue gown, valued at 40s., every two years. The Sisters had two rooms each and were supplied with fuel for fires.

To pay for this the Founder left £3,700 3 per cent Consuls, which brought in just over £100 a year. For the first century of its existence this appears to have been enough to manage on. John Baker says, 'It is reported that in 1902, income was £111 6s. 4d. and expenditure £109

66   The Parson brothers' almshouses founded 1796

5s. 6d.',[2] a situation which Mr. Micawber would have described as happiness; but extra expenses such as the provision of modern drainage in 1893 and roof renewal in 1908 caused great difficulty. In 1895, part of the garden was sold so that Onslow Road, which had taken the place of Love Lane, could be widened. In 1905 more of the garden was sold and the quarterly dinner days, when at least one Trustee and the Rector of Stoke dined with the Sisters, were stopped.

William Parson died in 1799, aged 73, and was buried with his brother Henry in the Old Churchyard at Stoke. (Where was their sister buried?) They are also commemorated in two brass memorials on the north wall of Stoke Church. Keeping these and the tomb in a state of good repair is a charge upon the Trust. The brothers' tomb can still be seen, with the simple inscription:

> In memory of Henry Parson late mercer and draper of Guildford who departed this life … 1791 aged 62 years. Also in memory of William Parson, late mercer and draper of Guildford and brother to Henry Parson, who departed this life … 1799 aged 73 years.

The Trustees at William's death were the Rector, the Rev. George West, William Bray of Shere, John Peyton Shrubb, Mr. James South and Mrs. Thomas Freaks, senior, of Guildford.

Mr. Palmer gives the names of those who continued to serve as co-operative Trustees under a new scheme worked out by the Charity Commissioners in 1908. Once state pensions had become established it was possible to ask the inmates for a contribution towards the maintenance of the Hospital, so that one solution of financial difficulties was to accommodate more people who would pay for maintenance charges. Between 1969-80 room was made for 12 women and a warden and in 1980 a 13th flat was provided by putting a first floor into the central chapel block.[3] Thus the interior has been extensively altered but the outside of the building has been preserved as it was when it was first built. John Baker writes, 'The windows remain unspoilt and add a quaint Gothic touch to an otherwise classical Georgian building.'[4] The front door into the chapel or hall remains, but is no longer used. The cupola with a clock and bell was necessary because the site in 1796 was an isolated one. On the external west wall of the Hospital and on the south gable there are mathematical tiles. These give the appearance of bricks but are not as expensive.[5]

Originally the six poor widows were to come from Stoke, or Worplesdon if Stoke could not supply the requisite number. Now there are 13 well-appointed, self-contained flats and a matron's cottage, and the occupants may be drawn from anywhere in the locality. It would seem that the intention of the Parson brothers has been carried out so that two centuries after its foundation it still provides a comfortable haven for widows or spinsters aged over 60.

Neither William nor Henry married and their sister Sarah did not marry either. However, they wanted to perpetuate their name and chose the line established by their half-brother Robert Trimmer. His daughter Elizabeth had married James Freaks of Moor House Farm, Farnham, and she had two sons, James and John. William called these two his nephews, made the Trustees of the Hospital their guardians and paid their school and university expenses. When they had been ordained and taken orders they were to 'leave and

67   Memorial inscription on a woolsack

68   Mathematical tiles on external west wall

69   The Parson brothers' table tomb in Stoke churchyard

discontinue the name of Freaks and use the name Parson only'.[6] It is this James Parson whose name was added to the brass memorial of his great-uncle Henry Parson when he died in 1827. James had nine children, four of whom were sons, and it was his eldest son, the Rev. William Henry Onslow Parson, who came by invitation and dined with the Trustees and Sisters at Stoke Hospital on the occasion of the centenary in 1896.

To mark the bicentenary there was a special cake, cut by the mayor, and two invaluable chair lifts have been installed.[7] The Parson brothers' Hospital is still adjusting to the new, while carrying on the ideals of the founders in the old building behind the wall in Stoke Road.

Stoke was the beneficiary of several charities, of which the Hospital was the most important, but was only marginally involved in the largest of all local charities—that established by Henry Smith.

The Henry Smith Charity

Henry Smith was born in Wandsworth, Surrey, in 1548. He became an alderman in the City of London and was probably a silversmith. He is known to have lived in Silver Street, Cheapside. He had no children, was a widower and knew of few relatives, and so 'determined to dispose of his wealth to charitable uses'. Before he died in 1627, he set up a Board of Trustees to administer his personal estate after his death, gave £1,000 each to a number of Surrey towns, and sanctioned the purchase for Guildford of land to be held by the Trustees so that 'the rents and profits should be received by the mayor and approved men … and equally divided among the poor'.

In fact, the area taken over by the Trustees, which included the Town Mills at the foot of Guildford High Street, was the area covered by the ancient manor of Poyle which had been given to Robert Testard by William the Conqueror and which, together with Stoke, had probably supplied the land on which the borough of Guildford was established. That the ancient manor of Poyle formed the bulk of the Henry Smith donation is supported by a book in the S.A.S. library *Collections relating to Henry Smith Esq. 1800*, printed by John Nichols, Red Lion Passage, Fleet Street. On pages 28-9 it lists the places acquired as a result of Smith's charity as laid down in the Court of Chancery on 19 April 1706: 'All the demesne lands of the manor of Poyle situate in the parishes of St Marie's [sic], St Nicholas and the Holy Trinity in Guildford and in Stoke, Worplesdon and elsewhere'.

Thus in Guildford the Smith Charity was always known as the Poyle Charity. Poyle manor included land scattered about Stoke—a manor's property was rarely confined within one block of land and maps of the 18th and 19th centuries record Poyle land: on the Ichnography of 1739, the Joseph's Lane map of 1812 and the Tithe Award Map of 1841. The rents paid by the people to whom these outposts of the manor of Poyle were leased would go to the Smith estate trustees for distribution to the poor of Guildford.

However, a little later Stoke itself benefited directly from the Henry Smith Charity when in April 1650 the Trustees allotted the rents from Smith's Warbleton estate in Sussex to a long list of places in Surrey, among them Stoke, which received £12 p.a. The next largest sum was to Woking with £10. The revenue from this, as with all Smith's charities, was to be given 'to and for the relief of aged poor and infirm persons, married persons having more children born in lawful wedlock than their labours can maintain, poor orphans … and infirm poor old people of good character'.[8] It could not be used for the relief of any 'persons given to excessive drinking, whoremongers, common swearers, pilferers or otherwise notoriously scandalous'.

In 1931, when Williamson's book on Guildford Charities was published he wrote: 'The sum usually received from the Smith Charity comes to about £40.' He also says, writing of the Henry Smith Charity in Guildford, that after the regular payments (of 7s. 6d. a week to 25 pensioners) had been made, the remainder went into an Emergency Fund. This was used for 'the benefit of necessitous poor persons of either sex of good character and resident in the Borough as it was in 1879'. This enlarged the scope of the charity to include the poor of Stoke Within Guildford, who had until 1835 been outside the Borough and therefore not eligible. Thus Stoke was also helped by the Smith Charity as indeed was nearly every place in Surrey.

There is a postscript to the workings of the Smith Charity which Williamson mentions, and Stoke being again indirectly involved it may be worth including.[9] The Trustees found that possession of the Guildford Town Mills was not an unmixed blessing. They were forced to go to court because Guildford complained that the water wheels at Guildford were reduced in power by the high level of water in the mill pool which they said was due to the Stoke Mill owners keeping an unauthorised head of water at their mills. The arbitrator gave a decision in favour of the Trustees and the Town Council. However the Trustees decided it would be simpler to sell the Town Mills to Guildford, which they did for the large sum of £6,000 in 1894.[10] The mills were then closed.

An Alchemist's Legacy

There were two Prices, uncle and nephew, who both left legacies for the poor of Stoke. The uncle, James Price, lived in Stoke in a house which, according to Williamson, later became the *Stoke Hotel* (now Finnegan's Wake). He left £400 to be invested and the revenue to be distributed to the poor by the rector and churchwardens of Stoke yearly on Christmas Day. He left the bulk of his fortune, which was considerable, to his nephew James, the son of his sister who had married James Higginbottom, on condition that nephew James adopted the surname Price.

The second James was born in London in 1752. He went up to Oxford and graduated in 1777 at the age of 25. His uncle died in 1781 and James Price II bought a large house in Stoke (Matthew Alexander suggests that it stood in the upper High Street or Stoke above Bars).[11] Here he set up a laboratory to experiment with the process of turning base metal into gold. In the same year he was elected a Fellow of the Royal Society. It is difficult to account for this. It was an honour which he had not yet earned. However, the very next year he announced that he had found the catalyst which would turn base metal into gold and he published a pamphlet entitled 'An account of some Experiments on Mercury, Silver and Gold made at Guildford in May 1782'. He proceeded to demonstrate to large numbers of people, including the Rev. Owen Manning (of Manning and Bray) and Lord Onslow that he could turn mercury and silver into gold. This was not for himself—his uncle had left him a fortune. In any case, it had cost him £17 to make £4 worth of gold, but he did not publicise this fact, nor would he disclose the nature of the catalyst. This secrecy infuriated Sir Joseph Banks, President of the Royal Society, who insisted that the experiments should be repeated before qualified chemists. This repetition took place in Stoke on 3 August 1783. Three chemists arrived and, while they were inspecting the apparatus, James Price either swallowed poison or was overcome by mercury fumes. In any case, he fell dead at their feet. The verdict at the inquest was, in the words of one of Price's neighbours, 'Lunacy upon general evidence of his having in many instances acted like a man insane'. Insanity meant that he was not guilty of suicide and could therefore be buried in St John's Church, Stoke. His memorial is inaccurate about the date of his death and also about his age. Perhaps the situation into which his ambition or his naiveté had led him did nearly drive him mad. But before his death he made a will by which the rector and churchwardens were to apply the income of the money bequeathed by him in the same way as they did the money received from his uncle's charity. In 1931 Williamson reported that the annual income of the two charities amounted to about £27.

There are three other benefactors of Stoke Parish. In 1828 William Attfield left £125 to be invested and the revenue used for the upkeep of the Parish Sunday School. At the time the will was drawn up in 1826 the school met in premises which had formerly been a public house called the Red Lion. In the event of there being no Sunday School in Stoke the income should be used to have the Gospel preached in the Meeting House in Worplesdon.

In addition to this, Williamson mentions the Upperton Charity of 1889 and the Field Charity of 1907. Both intended money to be made available for the upkeep of their graves but neither was a legally valid bequest and so in each case the money was administered by the rector and churchwardens for the benefit of the poor of the parish.[12]

Today

I am grateful to Mr. C.E. Fullagar, assistant clerk to the Trustees of Guildford Municipal Charities, for explaining the position of the Stoke Charities today. He lists four Stoke Charities: the charity consisting of the share of the Charity of Henry Smith (Warbleton Estate), James Price Charity, Dr. Price's Charity, Upperton Charity (but not Attfield). The income from these forms part of the Guildford Relief in Need Charities which provides assistance for people residing in the Borough of Guildford, the area of benefit being the Borough before the 1974 reorganisation of local government. Applications for help are made through Social Services, Health Visitors, Community Mental Health Teams, etc.

Whilst not being a major beneficiary from the Henry Smith Charity, as Guildford was, Stoke has nevertheless had its share of benefactors and a permanent memorial to their munificence in the shape of the Parson brothers' Hospital and in the list of benefactors whose gifts are today administered by the Trustees for the Guildford Municipal Charities.

Nine

Paynters and Parishes

Of all the rectors of Stoke, from William of Domesday onwards, the one who had the greatest effect on the Parish, because of the age in which he lived, was Francis Paynter. The Paynters were an ancient Cornish family tracing their ancestors back to Edward I. Francis' grandfather, also Francis, left Cornwall to make his fortune (very successfully) in London. Francis (grandfather) bought the Stoke advowson from George West who, according to Manning and Bray, had 'greatly improved the Parsonage House'. Francis intended the living for his son Samuel, who was ordained in 1826. In 1831 Samuel became Rector of Stoke and was installed by his father in Stoke Hill House, the 'greatly improved Parsonage House' apparently not being improved enough for Samuel. Stoke Hill House stood at the top of the hill on which the Bellfields estate has been built, with a magnificent view across the valley to Guildford. It was here that Sam's son Francis was born in 1836.

The family belonged to the Evangelical branch of the Anglican Church and were the friends of Henry Draper of Camden Chapel and of John Newton, the former slave trader. Francis went up to Trinity College, Cambridge, and was ordained in 1861. His father retired from Stoke in 1858 and Francis took over in 1862 at the age of 26. The intervening four years were covered by Richard Shepherd West.

Before becoming Rector of Stoke, Francis served for a year as curate to the Rector of Farnham, who placed him in charge of the Bourne area. Here he built his first chapel with funds from his father and friends. This chapel was the first of many that Francis was to build.

In 1864 Francis married Julia Ann, daughter of Major Porter. The two families met in Nice and Julia Ann, who came to Stoke in 1864, continued to live there until her death in her 100th year in 1939. Francis and Julia had eight children, of whom four survived infancy. Their eldest son, Francis Samuel, was born in 1865 and ordained in 1891. Ella married Major Treeby, Walter became a lawyer and Evelyn Mary married the Rev. Malcolm Archibald, Chaplain to the Royal Military College, Sandhurst. There was another daughter, Theodora, who was born in 1875 but she lived for only 11 years.

When Francis' father came to Stoke in 1831 the population numbered 788. Just over 30 years later, when Francis became Rector in 1862, he had 3,797 parishioners. When he resigned in 1897 the numbers had risen to over 14,000. His solution was to build. In 1867 the foundation stone of Christ Church was laid and in 1868 it was consecrated as a chapel of ease for those at the eastern end of the parish. That a chapel of ease was needed shows not only the extent of the original parish but also the enormous growth in the number of parishioners. They could no longer all squeeze into the parish church. The local paper reported that,

> The Church is from the design of Mr. Edward Christian, Messers. Swayne & Son, builders of Guildford, are the contractors ... It is to be regretted that the funds were not forthcoming to enable the committee to carry out the design of Mr. Christian in its entirety.

This would seem to savour of ingratitude, but it was a comment by a journalist, not the parishioners who were well-aware of the enormous contributions made by the Paynters, both

70   Stoke Hill House, the home of the Paynters

father and son, although the building did remain unfinished for some time. It was on his resignation in 1897 that Francis gave £600 for the completion of the tower.

In the 1870s the Army was reorganised, a new barracks was built at Stoughton, and in 1875 Francis Paynter became Chaplain. He gave a house in Barrack Road, known as the 'Soldiers Welcome', where soldiers could go to write letters and chat. But once again his congregations had enormously increased. It was probably this which triggered the building of two new churches at the other end of the parish from Christ Church. In 1876 the temporary iron church of St Saviour was put up in the Woodbridge Road at his own expense. In 1881 the third new church in the parish, Emmanuel, Stoughton, was begun in an iron room holding 300. In 1899 St Saviour's Church was consecrated and in 1902 Mrs. Paynter laid the Foundation Stone of the permanent Church of Emmanuel at Stoughton. Anne Sankey's book shows the handbill advertising this. The offertory, not surprisingly, was for the Building Fund and, as the ceremony took place on 24 February, 'A spacious tent will be provided and every possible precaution will be taken against cold and damp.'

In addition to the building of three new churches, Paynter gave money and energy to promoting the Total Abstinence Movement. He built the *Royal Arms Temperance Hotel* at the corner of Ward Street, a handsome building now belonging to the University of Surrey and occupied by the Bank of Scotland and Guildford Institute. He also built the Haydon Place Hall to be used as an educational centre for teetotal ideas and also built a number of coffee taverns, including one by Guildford Railway Station.

Education was another of his preoccupations. He played a part in the foundation of the High School by setting free his parish hall in Haydon Place and asking Miss Morton to establish a high school there, which was done in 1888. It was soon taken over by the Church Schools Company and became the school for daughters of the Establishment, including the Paynter daughters.

In the local directory of 1863, Stoke Parochial School is recorded as having been founded in 1856 'for affording a sound education to the children of the poor belonging to the parish at 2d. a week. It is supported by yearly subscriptions and contributions, annual sermons being preached on its behalf.' There were separate schools for girls, boys and infants and in *Vintage Guildford* there is an engaging photograph of Stoke Infants Class III taken *c*.1909. In 1891 the directory records that 'the weekly payments are regulated by the earnings of parents', and goes on, 'there is also a mixed school at Stoke Hill'. Francis Paynter's obituary notice in the *Surrey Advertiser* notes that he was a substantial contributor to the maintenance of the Stoke Church Schools. 'He saved our schools. Not only did he give £500 on his resignation to relieve them of debt but he came handsomely to the rescue on three or four occasions.'

As a staunch supporter of the Evangelical Movement, he was the originator and chairman of the Guildford Conventions. The first of these was held in June 1890 in the grounds of Stoke Hill House—its aim, the deepening of spiritual life and understanding. The missionary oak at Stoke Hill beneath which the members gathered became an important symbol and there is also reference to 'those glorious conventions under the tent in Foxenden Fields'. For those who

71 A photograph of rather awestruck Stoke infants

would like to read more about these conventions there is a book in the Guildford Institute Library: *Life Radiant, some memorials of the Rev. Francis Paynter M.A.* by S.M. Nugent (Marshall Bros., Paternoster Row, no date).

In 1897 Francis decided to resign his position as Rector of Stoke. He was 61 and wanted to devote the remaining years of his life to missionary work. He travelled widely to India, Africa, Egypt and the Mediterranean and took part in several continental conventions. He sent a cheque for £1,000 to the Centenary Fund of the British and Foreign Bible Society, and he was a big yearly subscriber to home and foreign missionary societies.

He was succeeded at Stoke by Bishop Ingham (previously Bishop of Sierra Leone), who wrote of Francis:

> When a man who has been in spiritual charge for 34 years remains in the parish as a parishioner, lives in one of the biggest houses and wields the influence of an old county personality, a new rector may pardonably feel a little anxious. But it is only plain truth to say that from first to last, whether Mr. Paynter approved or disapproved of what was done, there was not even a suspicion of interference from Stoke Hill.

Not only did the churches for the new parishes have to be built but the parishes themselves

had to be properly constituted. This task was begun by Francis Paynter and completed by Bishop Ingham. In 1893 the 'Districts' of St Saviour, Guildford and Emmanuel, Stoughton were constituted by Order in Council. This was followed by the Stoke Church Extension Scheme, formed in 1897 to complete the creation of the 'New Parishes'. St Saviour's Church was consecrated in 1899 and Emmanuel in 1902. Christ Church, which had been consecrated first, was made a fully constituted Parish Church by Order in Council in 1936.

Samuel and Francis Paynter were the last to purchase or inherit the advowson of Stoke. It was they who decided to place the right to appoint to the benefice in the hands of the Simeon Trustees.

It was the enormous rise in the population of the area from under 4,000 to over 14,000, plus the building of the barracks at Stoughton, which made the division of the old, extensive parish of Stoke necessary. To build three new churches with the full complement of church halls was an enormous undertaking and probably would not have been achieved without the generosity and determination of Francis. In a letter to the editor of *Outlook* on the 'Division of Stoke Parish' the writer notes, 'Nearly £15,000 had been raised in eight years. A large portion ... had been the gift of the Rev. Francis Paynter.'

72 Memorial raised to Francis Paynter by his wife Julia Ann in the churchyard

73 Memorials to Francis Paynter in the church

He died unexpectedly on 13 January 1908 at Stoke Hill House where he had been born. He was in his 73rd year. The obituary notice in *Outlook* for 21 January 1908 observes,

> Although well advanced in years the deceased gentleman had displayed excellent vitality … as recently as Christmas Day last he preached at Stoke Church … Since then he had not appeared in his clerical capacity but had frequently walked and driven about the extensive grounds of Stoke Hill and the neighbourhood.

Julia Ann raised several memorials to her husband, two memorial tablets in the church, and an obelisk in Stoke Churchyard across the road from the church.

Ten

Breweries, Inns and Beershops

From Brewhouse to Temperance House

The production and consumption of beer have always been important occupations. While many households brewed their own beer, the Guildford area—partly because of the wool traders and partly because of its position on the route between London and Portsmouth—was well provided with inns, public houses and beer shops. Most of the information in this chapter on drinking places in Stoke has been drawn from Mark Sturley's book, *Breweries and Public Houses of Guildford*, published in 1990, the definitive work on this subject.

The brewery which lay in the angle between North Street and Chertsey Street was the one which took its name from Stoke. Mark Sturley says 'The Stoke Brewery first appears in the local directories in 1839 and 1840 when Thomas Chennell of 6, Woodbridge Road was named as the owner or occupant.' The Tithe map of 1841/2 shows that Thomas Chennell also had a brewery (and house) in Woodbridge Road, so it appears that he was running two breweries for a time until he concentrated on developing the Chertsey Street, North Square site. In North Square there was a convenient malthouse, older than the brewery, shown on the plan of the brewery *c.*1870 (Fig.10) in Mark Sturley's book. However, Mark can find no evidence that the brewery ever made use of the malthouse. The address of the brewery was usually given as 56 Chertsey Street, and the brewer's house was the redbrick building, now labelled 'Coffee Palace', fronting Chertsey Street (Vaughan House).

Thomas was not the only Chennell to be a miller and maltster. William purchased the Friary site and Henry built the flour mill there. Thomas seems to have been a successful brewer. In the Guildford Almanac of 1842, the *Star Inn* advertised 'Chennell's brilliant XXX and other ales'. Mark Sturley says that Chennell continued to appear in the directories as occupant of Stoke Brewery until 1848, although the 1847 Directory says that George Kettle, brewer and maltster, had moved from St Catherine's to Chertsey Street where he had erected a new brewhouse.

However, it was Thomas Bowyer who became the new owner of Stoke Brewery in 1853 and he remained there until he retired, probably in 1880, when his address was no longer 56 Chertsey Street but Waterden Road. During his time as brewer and maltster he always patronised the *White Hart* and he may well have been one of its suppliers. The beer consumed there was of a quality much appreciated by its consumers. Stoke Brewery was fortunate to have two such brewers as Thomas Chennell and Thomas Bowyer.

The latter was succeeded by his son Michael, who continued to run the brewery for another ten years (until 1890). Mark Sturley quotes several of Michael's advertisements; for example:

> Pure Malt and Hops
> M. Bowyer
> Stoke Brewery, Guildford

Begs the opportunity of thanking his numerous customers, and inform them he now has a stock of Pale Ales brewed in march from Malt and Hops alone, which are now in splendid condition.

Beer for Haymaking and Harvesting from 3d per gallon. 5 per cent discount allowed for cask.

Michael Bowyer's sister, Mary Frances, was married at Stoke Church in 1884 to John Stevens, son of William Stevens who owned the Wey Navigation. Thomas died in 1882 and was buried at Stoke, as was his wife Harriet on her death in 1895.

It was in that year that Miss Frances Olivia Vaughan founded the 'Workman's Home and Coffee Palace', its original name still splendidly blazoned across the front of the building. It was to provide a place for working men to go, away from 'the awful attractions of the public house'. So the building which had provided a family home for the brewers of Stoke became a temperance home for workmen. The Church Army took over the management of the home in 1950 and in 1984 the English Churches Housing Group became responsible for the premises. (For the work of Vaughan House today see Odds and Ends—Doss House, Chapter Twelve.)

74   Olivia Vaughan's Workman's Home and Coffee Palace

Pubs

Stoke, like Guildford, also had a plenteous supply of inns, pubs and beerhouses. Lying on a much-used route from London to the coast, not only were there travellers to be sustained, there were also frequent military movements, soldiers and sailors going to and from the ports. While these brought more customers, they also brought extra expense and uncertainty, for the forces had to be billeted as well as fed, and the government's settlement of its debts was extremely dilatory and often inadequate or non-existent. Moreover, the 'licentious soldiery' drove away more prosperous and therefore more profitable travellers. So the 18th century, a century of wars, became increasingly difficult for landlords and brewers. This was why a petition was drawn up asking that barracks should be built to house troops passing through the area. Details were added of public houses which had recently failed. Among the Stoke pubs were the *Blue Anchor* in Stoke above Bars (upper High Street) and the *Red Lion*. An inn called the *Red Lion* is shown on the Wey Navigation Map of 1923. It was near, or the predecessor of, the present *Forger and Firkin* in the Woodbridge Road.

There was no immediate response to the petition from the Government, but during the French Revolutionary Wars it was decided to build barracks throughout the country, in case of disorder at home. This elicited another petition from Guildford against the choice of the Friary site for the new barracks as being far too close to the centre of the town.

The number of inns and public houses in Stoke grew enormously in the 19th century, especially in the second half. This was partly because of the growth of population (see Chapter Nine) and partly because the Government encouraged the drinking of beer as a preferable

75 *The Spread Eagle*   **76** *The Prince Albert*, which still retains its original name

alternative to the dangerous consumption of cheap spirits. The Beerhouse Act of 1830, modified in 1834 and 1840, allowed any householder liable to assessment for the Poor Rate to obtain a licence to retail beer from his own dwelling. By the middle of the century 40,000 beerhouse licences had been issued countrywide and Stoke reflects this increase; in Mark Sturley's list of places licensed for the setting of beers, there are a large number established in Stoke around the middle of the century. The following are taken from Mark's list. A beershop at 9 Chertsey Street was occupied by William Goodman in 1840, then by William Savage, a greengrocer (the beershop was often in addition to some other occupation); Mrs. Savage was in charge in the 1860s and 1870s. There was also the *Golden Lion* at 4 Chertsey Street, and the *Leopard* at 12. The *Dolphin* at 57 lasted until 1964 and the *Spread Eagle* is still there. If one needed to quench one's thirst, Chertsey Street was a good place to make for! Continuing along into Stoke Road there is the *Stoke Hotel*, the *Prince Albert*—both still there—and the *Rifle Volunteer*, which was licensed in 1863 and continued until 1907, when it became a fish and chip shop. There is also the *King's Head* in nearby Kings Road.

Moving to Stoke Fields, there was the *Garibaldi* Beershop at 25, and at 88 the *Happy Man* Beerhouse. The whereabouts of the *Queen Victoria* Beershop in Stoke Fields has never been identified, and there were a number of beershops which never acquired a name but the Live and Let Live is still there in North Place.

A number of Stoke's inns have (or had) names which suggest when and why their names were chosen. The *Prince Albert* dates from the 1850s when the Prince Consort was most active. The *Drummond Arms*, built in Woodbridge Road in 1852 by James Smith, a builder who was

77 A pub that has changed its name (from the *Stoke Hotel*). It may also have been the home of Mr. James Price, uncle of the alchemist

also responsible for building the *Rats' Castle* and the *Napoleon*, recalls Henry Drummond who was not only M.P. for West Surrey but was also the purchaser of Albury Mansion, a powerful supporter of the Catholic Apostolic Church founded by Edward Irving and the builder of two new churches. The *Elm Tree*, which formerly opened on to York Road, was named after the avenue of elms that once led from the site of the Dominican Friary. The *Drummond Arms* is now called the *Forger and Firkin* and the *Elm Tree* is now the *Tap and Spile*. This renaming of inns hides any clue as to their history and identity.

However, under whatever name they exist, many of Stoke's inns have survived while Guildford's great inns, except for the *Angel* in the High Street have disappeared. Once they stood on the direct route between London and the south coast, a journey which took two days, with

78 A pub dating from the 1860s

a break at Guildford, before the coming of the railways. They had room to stable horses in the long premises going down to Lower Backside, 'near 200 horses' in the case of the *Red Lion*. But there is no room for stabling cars and lack of parking space, as well as all the other economic pressures, have destroyed the great inns which fronted Guildford's High Street, while Stoke's less prestigious inns are still there after 100 to 150 years.

But where are the ancient inns of Stoke? Originally, there were two *Dolphins*, one in Stoke above Bars, marked on the Iconography of Guildford in 1739, the other at 57 Chertsey Street in the angle made by Chertsey Street and North Street. This was a timber-framed and jettied construction belonging to the 16th century or earlier, so both the *Dolphin* inns had a long history. However, they would have drawn most of their customers from Guildford. There must have been an inn nearer Stoke Church and the mansion house to the south of the river. Attempts in the Surrey History Centre to discover where it was have not been successful. The most likely candidate is the building described in Chapter Three and because of long-standing tradition that this was at one time a pub an ancient board proclaims it to be an 'Ancient Jacobean Hostelry'. What is needed now is documentary evidence to support this.

Eleven

Some Vanished Maltings

Not only did people drink beer in inns, public houses and beerhouses, they also drank it at home, so the owners of properties of any size had their own brewhouse. Some also had their own malthouse, but this was not so common because the malthouse took up a good deal of room and the conversion of barley into malt requires great skill.

There had to be a steeping cistern to wash and soak the barley. There had to be a growing floor over which the barley was spread and on which germination took place. Then at precisely the right moment it had to be dried in the kiln or on the drying floor. A feature of malthouses was the louvres in the roof which could be controlled so that the maltster could achieve exactly the right temperature for germination and drying. It is on the malting process that the quality of the beer depends.

The large number of public houses in the Guildford area meant that malthouses would be needed. Most breweries had their own malthouse. Thomas Bowyer at Stoke Brewery was described in the Post Office Directory of 1877 as Thomas Bowyer and Son, Malt Merchants. On the other hand, a maltster might set up an independent maltings, not attached to a brewery.

There was another branch of the Bowyer family in Stoke, at Stoke Mill. In 1855, only a couple of years after Thomas acquired the brewery, the brothers Frederick and Henry Bowyer took over the corn mill and not far from this mill was a building which is marked on the Tithe Award Map as Malthouse Cottages, owned by Mr. George Smallpiece. The Wey Navigation Map of 1823 shows that Mr. Smallpiece was there almost 20 years earlier. (George or his father? Was he the founder of Stoke Malthouse?)

On the 1841 Census list the name Malthouse Row appears, occupied mainly by agricultural labourers and their families. In 1851, the heading becomes Stoke Malthouse Buildings and the first two heads of families recorded are John Mills, Baker, and James Mills, Labourer. By James Mills' name appear the words 'Row Barge'. In 1861 there is a long list of 17 households recorded as living in Stoke Malthouses.

In his invaluable collection of slides and photographs, Mr. Eric Hunter has a photo of a building standing near water and labelled 'Stoke Malthouse'. It seems probable that Eric's picture is of the malthouse that belonged to George Smallpeice and appears on the tithe map and the census lists.

A closer look at the 1823 map and the tithe map shows that the malthouse is both the right shape and in the right place to be the forerunner of the present *Row Barge Inn*. The name of the inn, having appeared in 1851, then drops out. This suggests that it was a small beerhouse being run by James Mills in tandem with his work as labourer. The earlier census lists refer to Stoke Malthouses, the later ones to cottages in Malthouse Lane. It looks as if the malthouse was divided into tenements and rented out. Judging by the number of people living there, it must have been a lucrative enterprise for the Smallpeices.

Mark Sturley, quoting Allen Batchelor, says that when F. A. Crooke & Co. acquired the *Row Barge* in 1909 it was described as 'All that messuage and beerhouse known by the name of

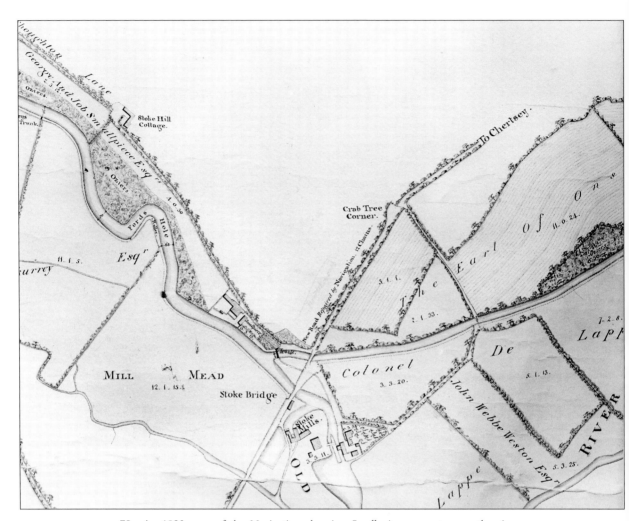

79   An 1823 map of the Navigation showing Smallpeice property near the river

80   Stoke Malthouse (Dennis May's impression of Eric Hunter's postcard)

the Row Barge recently rebuilt … three cottages on one side and six on the other which with five others have been pulled down'. Here is evidence of the numerous cottages into which the old maltings had been divided and the re-emergence of the old name of the small beerhouse mentioned in 1851. In 1881 George Cassell had a public house in Malthouse Lane, but the name is not given.

Sit outside the *Row Barge Inn* today and look at the shape of the property by the riverside. It is the same as the shape of the property shown on the two maps and the relationship of the inn to Stoke Mill and the river is right. The

81 Towards the *Row Barge Inn*

rebuilding of the *Row Barge* means that there is no physical evidence of the maltings left but there is no doubt that the inn stands on the site of Stoke Malthouse.

Nor is there any doubt that the former maltings were a centre of occupation and activity. In 1851 there are at least two paper makers labourers, and at Paper Mill House lived George Feller (and his family). His occupation was paper maker and his place of birth was Germany. Among the occupations mentioned in the 1881 census are mangle woman, bargeman, cleaner on railway, signalman on railway, railway guard and flour mill carter. The railway was growing in importance. It had arrived in 1845 and the new London Road—Cobham line was opened in 1885, but bargemen were still needed. Several of them lived in Malthouse Lane. The corn

82 *The Row Barge Inn*

83 Waterways near the miller's house

84 The 17th-century miller's house with pigeon loft, referred to in the 1851 census as Paper Mill House

mill was still in action, although by 1881 the paper makers had gone. Among the other inhabitants of the old maltings were a butler, a printer and compositor, and a drain pipe trimmer. The variety of jobs is fascinating.

On the Tithe Award Map the Mangles estate shows no sign of either a brewhouse or a malthouse, but the Surrey History Centre archives contain a document which deals with the sale of 'Malthouse Yard and hereditaments' by various Mangles, including Mary Mangles of Woodbridge Cottage, widow, to Thomas Drewett the younger son of Nicholas, yeoman, for £870. The date of the document is 28 September 1839. James Mangles had died the year before. The description of the property is as follows: 'All that Malthouse with the drying kiln, Coke Oven, Yard and premises thereto belonging ... in the occupation of Thomas Taunton ... on the west by the Wey Canal.' Thomas Taunton erected the Castle Brewery before his death in 1839. His son, also Thomas, set up the Cannon Brewery and public house and was later involved in the Friary Brewery so one is not surprised to find them in occupation of a malthouse. The Mangles document (BR/T/976/1) also has a diagram map showing, in addition to the malthouse, a coke oven, the coal yards and wharf, belonging to the trustees of the late James Mangles. It is a pity that the maps do not show where this property stood. It is the second vanished malthouse in this part of Stoke.

Twelve

Odds and Ends:
A Mud House, a Mad House, a Doss House and a Gallows

Stealing the Common from the Goose

Documents have survived which show Nathaniel Hillier to have been determined to assert his rights and prevent encroachment on the wastelands of the manor. Two who attempted such encroachment were firmly dealt with. In 1806 Joseph Erwood admitted that he had 'committed a trespass on the waste of the manor of Stoke next Guildford by erecting a cottage thereon without the consent of Nathaniel Hillier Esqr, the Lord of the said manor'.[1] His plea continues:

> I entreat the said Nathaniel Hillier Esqr to forgive the offence I have committed against him and not to compel me to pull down the said cottage but to grant me his authority to hold and retain the same … on my making such acknowledgement by way of fine or quit rent … as he shall think proper to demand as Lord of the Manor of Stoke.

The sum agreed by way of fine or quit rent was obviously acceptable since Joseph Erwood did not have to demolish his newly built cottage. John Marsh was not so fortunate.

> I do hereby acknowledge that I have committed a trespass on the waste of the manor … by beginning to erect a mud cottage on a part thereof without the consent of the lord of the said manor by whose orders I have been obliged to pull it down again and level all to the ground.

He goes on:

> Now I hereby entreat Nathaniel Hillier Esqr to forgive the offence I have committed against him [this seems to have been the accepted formula in this situation] and permit me to erect the said cottage (for myself my wife and three children) on such part of the waste of his said manor as he shall think fit.

Permission was given to erect the said 'mud cottage' at Slyfield Green. It was incidents such as these, occurring all over the country, which led to the following well-known doggerel appearing in the *Tickler Magazine* on 1 February 1821:

> The fault is great in man or woman
> Who steals a goose from off a common
> But what can plead that man's excuse
> Who steals a common from the goose.

In 'A survey of the parish and manor of Stoke belonging to Nathaniel Hillier Esqr 1801', the new Lord of the Manor lists the 'Wastelands etc. within the manor of Stoke' as follows:

> Gomer Green or Slyfield Green
> Woodbridge Common and wastes adjoining
> New Pond Common. Roads and wastes adjoining thereto.

There was, in fact, very little waste land in Stoke compared with other manors in Surrey.

The Mad House

Mad House Lane, which ran from the dog leg in Woodbridge Road straight up to Chertsey Street, took its name from the lunatic asylum in Leapale House, on the right hand side of the

I Joseph Erwood do hereby acknowledge that I have committed a Trespass on the Waste of the Manor of Stoke next Guildford Surrey by erecting a Cottage thereon without the Consent of Nathaniel Hillier Esq.ʳ the Lord of the said Manor —

I intreat the said Nathaniel Hillier Esq.ʳ to forgive the Offence I have committed against him, and not to compel me to pull down the said Cottage, but to grant me his Authority to hold and retain the same for my own Use and Benefit, on my making such Acknowledgment by Way of Fine or Quit-Rent to the said Nathaniel Hillier Esq.ʳ as he shall think proper to demand as Lord of the Manor of Stoke — Witness my Hand this fifteenth Day of July in the Year of our Lord, one Thousand Eight Hundred and Six,

J. Erwood

85 Petition to Nathaniel Hillier Esqʳ. not to order the pulling down of a cottage built without his permission on the waste of the manor of Stoke

lane going up from Woodbridge Road. It is not known when this asylum came into existence, but the earliest candidate for the position of founder is David Irish.

In 1701 he published a book in two parts: *Advice concerning Physic* and *Discourse touching Astrology*. Nearly two and a half centuries later, in July 1939, Dr. Williamson wrote in *Guildford City Outlook*, that a Mr. Currington had kindly permitted him to inspect 'a copy of a most interesting and unusual book in two parts'. This was the book by David Irish, published in Swan Lane, Guildford in 1701. Dr. Williamson wrote an account, based on this book, of the life of David Irish under the title *An Eighteenth Century Guildford Medical Man*, and asked 'Can any correspondent tell us in what house the learned quack resided?' No one could, but reading of the particular interests of 'the learned quack', it seems quite possible that it was he who was responsible for the institution of the Mad House.[2]

According to Dr. Williamson, the author termed himself 'David Irish, Practitioner in Physics and Chirurgery at Stoke near Guildford' and claimed to be expert in every branch of medicine. He said that he had an invaluable antidote against smallpox and discusses at length 'the cure of melancholy phrensie and madness'. He claimed to be a skilled dentist and to be capable of performing every kind of operation. He preferred to receive patients into his own house and while he spent certain times in Thorpe, Chertsey and Farnham, his H.Q. appears to have been Stoke. 'My house at Stoke, just by Guildford is situate in a wholesome air and is in every way convenient for the reception of any person of what quality soever" … 'I was born and baptised in Weekham … but God knows where I shall lay my bones.'[3]

There is no doubt that he laid them in Stoke. There is a memorial to him and his family in Stoke church; and it is not impossible that his house 'just by Guildford … in wholesome air' was the origin of the Mad House. He liked to receive people he was treating to board in his home, and given his interest in 'melancholy phrensie', may well have filled his house with lunatics.

The next candidate for the post of founder of the Mad House is Caleb Woodyer. There is definite evidence that he owned the Mad House. Caleb became partner of William Newland Junior in 1811. In the Quarter Sessions Minutes Books for 1837-8, there is notice of a licence issued to Caleb Woodyer, surgeon, to keep Leapale House in Stoke next Guildford for the reception of insane persons, male and female. Numbers were limited to 20 and the licence was to last for 13 months from 3 July 1838. At the end of that period it was renewed, but issued this time to Mr. Stephen Golding.[4] Mr. Golding was probably Caleb Woodyer's assistant because Caleb appears again in 1841, both on the Tithe Award Map and in the census list. On the tithe map he is shown as the owner and occupier of Leapale House, garden and buildings lying on the south side of Mad House Lane; and the census shows that there were five male and four female lunatics in Leapale House.

Mrs. Green, in her *Sidelights on Guildford History*, says that the asylum was run by old Dr. Sells, and Mr. Bateman in his *RamblingRecollections of Old Guildford* follows her in this and adds that Dr. Sells acquired the sinister nickname of 'Butcher' Sells. He did not begin his work in Guildford until 1841, but he must have taken over the asylum after Caleb Woodyer.

The Mad House continued to appear in the census lists certainly until 1871, when there were five patients, two attendants and a nurse, although the lane had become Leapale Lane in the 1870 Town Plan. However, by the 1880s an engineering company had moved in while in, the 1891 census Leapale House is inhabited by Mary Rushbrook living on her own means. So the Mad House disappeared in the 1870s.

Both Mrs. Green and Mr. Bateman say that the Mad House may later have become Mrs. Tye's school for young ladies, but in the census return of 1871, Mary Tye is the Head of Sandfield House Academy with Martha Tye (sister-in-law) and Mary and Catherine Tye (daughters) all school mistresses. In the 1891 census Catherine Tye was principal of a girls' school with 15 boarders but her school, though in Leapale Lane, was at Stoke House, so it would seem that the Tyes' school for young ladies did not move into the former Mad House.

Eventually the property was sold to William Pimm, head of the furniture and upholstering firm, and his son Laurence Pimm sold it to the government for the Guildford Telephone Exchange, when the property was described as 'Leapale House and property in Leapale Lane, and, in addition, Ray's Lane, later called Haydon Place and 3, Martyr Road'. The land in Haydon Place was formerly part of the old Cherry Garden—a market garden.

Vaughan House

This was the home of Thomas Bowyer, the successful manager of Stoke Brewery from about 1852 until about 1880, and his son Michael, who continued to run the brewery until 1890.

In 1895 Miss Vaughan acquired the former home of the Bowyers and turned it into the 'Workman's Home and Coffee Palace'. It was a temperance home for workmen and has lasted for longer than the brewery, being now over a century old.

In 1984 it was taken over by the English Churches' Housing Group, at which time it provided a home for about 65 men. Speaking at the centenary meeting of the Surrey branch of the Friends of the Churches Housing Group, the mayor of Guildford, John Woodhatch, recalled cleaning windows at the house when he was a lad of 14. 'It was a frightening place in those days,' he said.

However, in 1991, after a tremendous fundraising effort on the part of the Church Housing Trust and with a grant from the Housing Corporation, Vaughan House, which had to be closed for a year to carry out the complete re-organisation, re-opened with separate bedrooms instead of steel walled partitions, and with shared kitchens, giving inmates more independence. It continued the work begun by Olivia Vaughan for those with alcohol problems and has extended its help to women in need. There is one flat available solely for women. The Workmen's House and Coffee Palace thus continues to do invaluable work while preserving its original name.[5]

Ganghill

The Surrey map by Senex in 1729, in addition to recording that 'Esq. Turner' was at Stoke, shows an area to the north east labelled 'Alden', with a house to the west of the road to London. This must be Aldham Farm, later known as Stoke Park Farm and now incorporated into Abbot's Wood estate. Opposite the house named Alden is another house, unlabelled standing, in a completely blank area to the east of the London Road. This is where Ganghill Farm stood, and the presence of a building is recorded by Senex though it is obvious that little else was known about the area. On the Rocque map of 1768, the area is marked Gangle Common to the west of London Road and Gangle Wood to the east, with farm buildings shown on both sides of the road. It appears again on the O.S. map of 1816, clearly marked Gang Hill, as it is on Greenwood's map of 1823. On a plan of Ganghill Farm in the Surrey History Centre (1320/23/1) (undated) the boundaries are given as 'bordering on John Dyson Esq.'s land on the west, Lord Onslow on the north and Ganghill Common on the east'. The farm had two fields in Worplesdon and two fields in Burpham in addition to Stoke, the farm being in the occupation of Mr. John Peché. The *Anchor Ale House* is marked on the plan as it is on the Greenwood map of 1823. At the time of the Tithe Award in 1841, Ganghill Farmstead was owned and occupied by Alexander Robertson, whose land bordered on Ganghill Common and Ganghill Wood, part of Delap's estate, the husband of Nathaniel Hillier's elder daughter. The Delap estate included a rope-walk.

Further proof that Ganghill was an old established area appears in a report on the Ganghill hangings which took place on 26 August 1776. This account comes from the *Surrey Advertiser* of 27 May 1977. Three men were hanged. One of them was Mr. James Potter, a highwayman. He robbed a man called William Calvet of 11 guineas and his watch. Potter was a coachman who lived at the *White Hart Inn*. The others who were hanged were Christopher Ellis, a burglar, and Frederick William Gregg convicted of robbery with violence. According to the original account, 'They were conveyed in a cart to Ganghill Common from the jail at 11 o'clock where they continued in prayer for half an hour. They all behaved penetant [sic] and were turned off'. Why a gallows was put into operation in the area of present-day Finches Rise it is difficult to say; perhaps the crimes were committed close by.

Thirteen
The Other Side of the Ditch

As has already been pointed out, the area covered by the borough of Guildford was remarkably small. To the north the boundary was Lower Backside, to which the yards, stables and gardens of the houses and inns lying on the north side of Guildford High Street sloped down. To the north, of Lower Backside, which became North Street, lay the North Town Ditch and beyond that lay the parish of Stoke.

From 1835 onwards, as a result of the Municipal Corporations Act, the areas of Stoke closest to the borough boundaries (and the north side of North Street could hardly be closer) were brought within the borough and known as Stoke Within. The Tithe map of

86 The market garden area of Stoke in 1881 (from Museum archives)

87 This was formerly a 'banqueting or summerhouse' in a walled garden in Stoke next Guildford

1841/2 records the situation at about this time and should show whether there was any crowding of the boundaries or ribbon development (of the kind which had occurred in Chertsey Street) in the area lying behind North Street from North Square to Woodbridge Road. This area was divided into almost equal quarters by Madhouse Lane crossing Frog Lane at right angles. Frog Lane ran from North Street down to a large area of arable land—Footpath Field and Exhibition Field, each of over six acres, and George Field of over two acres. The houses and terraces appear to have had plenty of space and much of the area consisted of gardens.

For instance, Joseph Haydon owned a large area on Frog Lane, now known as Haydon Place. It consisted of 'Garden and Greenhouse, etc.' as well as 'part of garden and cottage'. In the area behind North Square William Sparkes had 'a garden and Greenhouse, House, Smithy and yard'. Antony Lee owned property to the northwest of Madhouse Lane described as 'Garden and Summerhouse', occupied by Edward Filmer. Across the lane was the large garden of Leapale House. Other properties were East Sandfield House and West Sandfield House, both with large gardens, and to the west the extensive 'Garden, House and Grounds' of John Peto Shrubb. There was also the garden and paddock of Caleb Woodyer backing on to Joseph Haydon's property, and John Martyr had an extensive market garden worked by William Peters. There was no Leapale Road.[1]

So it looks as if there was little development of this area before 1835. It remained rural and horticultural, although there was Thomas Chennell's brewery in Woodbridge Road. On the other side of Woodbridge Road were meadows running down to the river owned mainly by Lord Onslow or George Smallpeice and his wife Elizabeth, who owned the Leas and Garden.

As to how much development there was after 1841/2, the 1870 Town Plan indicates what differences there were.

One obvious change was that Leapale Road had been carved out, with Leapale Terrace filling the gap between the Telegraph Post and the County and Borough Halls, both new buildings, as was the large County Police Station. The Churchacre Iron Works had taken the place of Antony Lee's 'Garden and Summerhouse', while north of the Friary Brewery lay the Gas Works and the Bone Mill. Frog Lane had become Ray's Lane and Madhouse Lane had become Leapale Lane, but the number of houses had not greatly increased, and it is surprising not to find a fully developed Ward Street considering that the Rev. John Ward, Rector of East Clandon, had acquired a yard and barn immediately to the north and laid out Ward Street and Martyr Road, named after his wife who was a daughter of John Martyr. Given that there was a time lag in the production of the Town Plan so that it records the position in 1868 rather than 1870, it is still surprising that the area was not more developed. The map shows numerous greenhouses behind North Square. It remained what it had long been—a market garden called the Cherry Garden.

However, the north side of North Street gave room to a number of Victorian buildings which are recorded in *Guildford As It Was* by Matthew Alexander. The photograph of North Street in the 1870s shows a wide, pleasant street. No wonder the weekly cattle market was moved from the High Street to North Street in 1865—there was so much more room.

In the 1840s a Methodist church was built on the corner of Woodbridge Road and North Street. Again, *Guildford As It Was* has a photograph and points out the manse for the minister, next door, with stabling for one horse. 'William Haydon donated a barrel-organ that played hymns and was manipulated vigorously by a blacksmith who lived in Stoke Fields.' However, this first church was too small for its flourishing congregation and a much larger church was completed in 1894.

In 1861 the huge County and Borough Halls were erected on the corner of Leapale Road and North Street. This was a multipurpose building: there were law courts for the Assizes and Petty Sessions; there were cells for prisoners; there was accommodation for the Guildford Institute and the Working Men's Institution. The *White Hart* lost many of its banquets to the Borough Halls and in 1912 the large hall, which could hold 1,000 people, was converted into the Theatre Royal.

In 1863 the Congregational Chapel was built at the corner of Leapale Road, opposite the Borough Halls. The building was begun in February and finished in September, thanks to the energy and determination of the Rev. John Hart.

One of the first buildings designed by Henry Peak after becoming Guildford's first Borough Surveyor still stands on the corner of Haydon Place and North Street. It was the *Surrey Arms*, built in 1865 as an outlet for Richard Elkins' North Street Brewery. However, it is no longer an inn, having become a pizza fast-food restaurant in the 1980s.

The fire station was originally a shed to house the horse-drawn, manually-pumped fire engine provided by Councillor Frank Apted in 1863. His daughter, Mrs. Broad, provided a new fire station in 1872 which lasted until another site was found in Ladymead in 1937. The North Street Fire Station now houses public toilets.

The *Royal Arms Temperance Hotel* was built by the Rev. Francis Paynter, determined to provide a centre for non-alcoholic refreshment. Lord Onslow laid the foundation stone in 1880 and opened it in 1881. The hotel side was a failure, and in 1891 the bedrooms on the upper floors were taken over by the Guildford Working Men's Institution. The café, however, continued until 1964. In 1892 the Guildford Working Men's Institution and the Guildford Institute combined and made the *Royal Arms* their headquarters. In 1982 they became the Guildford Institute of the University of Surrey, still housed in the handsome building on the corner of Ward Street and North Street, opposite the former fire station.

Behind this Victorian façade lived the inhabitants of Stoke Within Guildford, some more splendidly than others, as a document of 2 April 1875 shows. By this, the Rev. E.J. Ward conveyed the following property to Richard Sparkes:

> All that said messuage or tenement, formerly a Banquetting or Summerhouse lying in Stoke next Guildford erected in a garden adjoining the North Town Ditch then called North Street on the south side thereof and which said garden was bounded by the buildings formerly belonging to Mr. Gilham and then to the said Edward John Ward on the east, the garden formerly in the occupation of Richard Kennett and then of Charles Hart belonging to the Congregation of Dissenters called Baptists on the north and the Barn and Yard formerly of Mr. Shudell and then of Mrs. Elkins with a lane leading from Guildford to Stoke called Frog Lane on the west which was purchased by John Child deceased from Richard Young and was by John Child walled round.[2]

So here in Stoke was a pleasant walled garden sheltering a summer house so desirable that it can be described as a Banquetting House. Life in Stoke was not without its refinements.

The occupations of the inhabitants of Stoke were mainly agricultural, surrounded as it was by farms, but there were also wheelwrights, millers, maltsters, brewers, innkeepers, paper makers and all those involved with canal traffic and, later, the railways. There were numerous schools and schoolmistresses reflecting the lack of choice of careers for women. There were also the many jobs provided in the households of the gentry. Stoke Park in the 1891 census had a butler, a footman, a cook, a lady's maid, a laundry maid, three housemaids, a kitchenmaid and a scullerymaid. The stableman lived over the stables. Woodbridge Park and Woodbridge House were similarly provided. There were also numerous horse keepers in North Street and Stoke Road in 1841. Henry Prosser, drawing master, lived in Stoke Fields.

A Letter from an Inhabitant of Stoke

Whatever the circumstances which led to the formation of Guildford, there is no doubt that the borough boundaries enclosed only a very small area. That Stoke was only just the other side of the North Town Ditch has already been pointed out. Similarly, the Grammar School lay only just within the borough boundary. The area to the east of the School had always been called Stoke above Bars and continued to be so called after it became part of Stoke Within. These limited boundaries meant that it was inevitable that any expansion by the borough of Guildford was bound to be at the expense of Stoke.

The wonder is that Stoke preserved its identity for so long (in fact for over a thousand years). There is plenty of evidence for this in the documents that remain (or were lost). In support of this enduring independence is Lady Britton's letter written to John Baker on 1 February 1983 and preserved in the Stoke file in the museum archives:-

> ... and cannot resist letting you know how much I agree with what you had to say last week about Stoke in general and Stoke Rd. in particular.
>
> I was born in Park Rd. in October 1900 and lived there for the first ten years of my life ... When I was a child, Stoke was very much a complete community, our postal address was 'Stoke-next-Guildford'. The present fried fish shop was still a public house called the '*Rifle Volunteer*'. The corner shop of Stoke Road and Park Rd. was a baker's, who baked his own bread on the premises; the opposite corner shop was a butcher's, and there were two small drapers' shops in Stoke Rd. besides one at the bottom end of Park Rd. The present sub-post office and off licence premises were occupied by Yorks, a good class grocers, while at the junction of Park Rd. and Drummond Rd. there was a general shop, which incorporated a butcher's, grocer's and baker's. Pigs were finally housed and slaughtered in a small area at the back of this shop and bread was also baked here in a brick oven fired by wood faggots. On Sundays, people who wished to have a hot roast dinner and also attend church used to pay ½d. to have their meat cooked in this oven, afterwards collecting it in time for the meal.
>
> There was a coachbuilder's work place in Park Rd. itself and next door to it a working blacksmith's complete with forge. Lamps were still lighted by lamplighters with a pole; barrel organs were pushed round to provide musical entertainment, and summer dust laid by a sprinkling water cart. Your drawing and article brought these things strongly to my recollection.

Notes

Nearly all the documents made use of here were found either in the Guildford Muniment Room or in the Local Studies Library, Guildford. However, all Surrey archives are now housed in the Surrey History Centre in Woking. Therefore any documents listed here will be found in the S.H.C. unless otherwise indicated.

My secondary source has been Manning and Bray: The History and Antiquities of the County of Surrey, 3 volumes 1804-14. Most of the references to Stoke are in vol.I published in 1804. This and the Surrey Archaeological Collections are to be found in the Surrey Archaeological Society Library.

The following abbreviations are used in the notes:

M&B   Manning and Bray
VCH   *Victoria County History*
S.A.S.   Surrey Archaeological Society
SAC   *Surrey Archaeological Collections*
DNB   *Dictionary of National Biography*
HMSO   Her Majesty's Stationery Office

Chapter 1 Early History

1. *SAC* vol.XI, p.250
2. Found by Mr. Shettle of the Fire Service
3. *Oxford Book of Place Names*, p.425
4. *Place Names of Surrey* (1934), pp.150-1
5. *Early Medieval Surrey*, John Blair, (Alan Sutton and SAS 1991), p.97
6. *Ibid.*, p.104
7. *Story of Stoughton by Pen and Camera* (1910), p.19. There is a copy of this in the SAS Library
8. M&B vol.I, p.169
9. The Calendar of the Liberate Rolls 33 Henry III, p.51, HMSO
10. *Ibid.*, p.374
11. *VCH* vol.3., p.562
13. M&B vol.I, pp.19-20
14. M&B vol.I, p.168

Chapter 2 Parish Church, St John the Evangelist

1. Guildford Archaeology Group Newsletter, 13 December 1985, p.4. Can be found in the *SAC* Library
2. *VCH* III, pp.372-3

3. Pevsner, *Surrey*, p. 272 note
4. John Blair, *Early Medieval Surrey*, p.105
5. John Blair, 'Surrey Endowment of Lewes Priory Before 1200', *SAC* vol.LXX (1980), pp.97-126
6. John Blair, *Early Medieval Surrey*, p.106
7. D.M. Sturley, *Royal Grammar School, Guildford*, pp.59-60
8. M&B vol.I, p.182
9. 1320/9/13,14
10. These may be found at the S.H.C.
11. Graham, Thomas William, *Some Account of the Parish of Stoke Next Guildford and its Church* (1933), pp.14-16
12. *SAC* vol.51, p.93
13. Henry Peak's Note Books, Guildford, p.344

Chapter 3 Waterways and Mills

1. Shirley, Corke, *The Wey and Godalming Navigations. A Short History*
2. 'Weston and the Cut at Stoke Mill', *SAC* vol.LXVI, pp.36-9
3. *Surrey History* vol.IV, no.1, p.54
4. *Ibid.* vol.III, no.1, p.12
5. P.A.L.,Vine, *London's Lost Route to the Sea*, David & Charles, Macdonald (1965), p.10
6. Corke, *op. cit.*, p.35
7. *Ibid.*, p.37
8. *SAC* vol.62, 'Wey Navigation Claims of 1671', pp.94-108
9. Corke, *op. cit.*, p.9
10. *Surrey History* vol.IV, no.1, p.54
11. H.E.S. Simmons has collected invaluable information about Surrey Mills. His work may be found in the research section of the SAS library
12. Henry Peak's Note Books, Guildford
13. *Surrey History* vol.IV, no.1, p.54
14. At the SHC
15. *Surrey Advertiser*, 1 September 1989: 'Stoke Mill Let for Record Rent'

Chapter 4 The Village

1. M.& B. vol.I, p.169
2. 1320/23/12
3. 1320/16/2 (13)
4. BR/ST/9, p.14
5. BR/ST/9, p.56
6. BR/ST/9, p.79
7. John Baker, 'Article on the old Inn at Stoke', *Surrey Advertiser*, 20.5.67
8. Guildford Archaeology Group, *Newsletter* no.21 (1993), p.27.
9. 1320/9/34,36
10. 1770/1-6
11. Russell, *History and Antiquities of Guildford*, pp.175-9
12. G.96/1/111
13. Wey Navigation map 1823. At S.H.C.
14. G.129/41/5

15. 1320/16/2 (1-50)
16. 1320/16/2 (1)
17. 1320/16/2 (8)
18. 1320/16/2 (8)
19. G.129/41/5
20. 1320/16/2/(61)
21. Q.S.2/1/34, pp.607 and 640
22. Q.S.2/1/35, pp.648-9

Chapter 5 Stoke Park, the Nabobs and Their Successors

1. M&B vol.1, p.169
2. 1320/11/20
3. *Ibid.*
4. John Baker, 'Stoke Park Mansion', *Surrey Advertiser*, Jan 1976
5. From notes by G.M.A. Beck, former archivist, in the Stoke File in Guildford Museum
6. Richard Wenger, 'The Story of Stoke', *Surrey Advertiser*, 16.5.81
7. *DNB* vol.XVIII, p.435
8. *Ibid.* p.437
9. *DNB* vol.VI, pp.299-301
10. M&B vol.I, p.168
11. *Ibid.*, p.169
12. 1320/6/2 (61)
13. G.129/41/6 1&2
14. BR/ST/9, p.75
15. For the cultural side of life at Stoke Park at the end of the 18th century I am indebted to Mr. Richard Wenger's two articles which appeared in the *Surrey Advertiser* on 2 and 16 May 1981.
16. From notes by G.M.A. Beck, former archivist, in the Stoke File in Guildford Museum.
17. BR/T/1012/1
18. E.R. Chamberlin, E.R., *Guildford*, (Macmillan, 1970), p.32
19. For further information see Mary Mackey's article in *Surrey History* vol.IV, no.3, pp.170-5

Chapter 6 Boundaries, Courts and Census Lists

1. BR/OC/1/2 p. 1070
2. 893/1. I am grateful to Laurence Spring (Guildford Muniment Room) for drawing my attention to this lively document.
3. BR/OC/1/2, p.108
4. *Ibid.*, p.110
5. 1320/17/3
6. BR/ST/9, p.79
7. 1320/14/2
8. 1320/9/11
9. Ann Stoughton, 'Guildford People and Places', p.47
10. The Census lists may be seen in the SHC
11. From the Stoke File in Guildford Museum

Chapter 7 Woodbridge

1. M&B vol.I, p.173
2. *Ibid*.
3. *DNB* XXII, Supplement p.1008
4. I am very grateful to Peter Sagar, who gave me booklets and a tape which he brought back from his visit to Western Australia and which form the main source of information about the Stirlings.

Chapter 8 Benefactors and Beneficiaries

1. Quoted by Mr. Philip Palmer in his privately printed paper on Stoke Hospital and its founders (1916).
2. John Baker, 'Parsons' Hospital' *Surrey Advertiser*, 28.1.83
3. Information supplied by Barlows Solicitors, Quarry Street, Guildford
4. John Baker, *op. cit.*
5. *Ibid*.
6. Philip Palmer, *op. cit.*
7. *Surrey Advertiser*, 1996
8. Collections relating to Henry Smith Esq.
9. C. George Williamson, *Guildford Charities*, (Corporation of Guildford, 1931)
10. *SAC* vol.74 (1983), Matthew Alexander, *The Mills of Guildford*, p.98
11. The story of the Alchemist, by Matthew Alexander, is to be found in the Stoke File in Guildford Museum.
12. C. George Williamson, *op. cit.*

Chapter 9 Paynters and Parishes

Information in this chapter comes from Henry J.Burkitt, *The Story of Stoughton by Pen and Camera*, 1910; Ann Sankey, Stoughton, *Guildford People and Places*; leaflets in the church; obituary notice of Francis Paynter in the Surrey Advertiser; S.M. Nugent, *Life Radiant: some memories of the Rev Francis Paynter M.A.* (A copy of this book is in the Guildford Institute library). Other sources are given in the text.

Chapter 11 Some Vanished Maltings

Census lists and maps are available in SHC.

Chapter 12 Odds and Ends

1. 1320/4/6. I am grateful to Shirley Corke, former archivist, for telling me about the mad house.
2. Dr. Williamson's article in the *Guildford City Outlook* was in the Local Studies Library: now in the SHC.
3. This may be an eccentric spelling of Wickham. There is a Wickham in Hampshire and one in Berkshire (but no Weekham).
4. Q.S.2/1/56 and Q.S.2/1/57. I am grateful, as ever, to Shirley Corke for supplying this information.
5. From 'The success story of Vaughan House', *Surrey Advertiser*, Dec 1995

Chapter 13 The Other Side of the Ditch

1. The Tithe map of 1841/2 is available in the SHC

Index

References which relate to illustrations only are given in **bold**.